FATE IS A MOUNTAIN

FATE IS A MOUNTAIN

By Mark W. Parratt

Smitty Parratt and Monty Parratt

All photos courtesy Parratt family archives.

Published by:
Sun Point Press
P.O. Box 4711
Whitefish, MT 59937
sunpointpress.com

ISBN 0-615-22987-4

Manufactured in the United States of America
First Edition/First Printing

DEDICATION

This book is dedicated to my brother, Monty Parratt, partner and best friend, whose heart and soul drove this writing project. The memory of his smiling face and his love will always be with me. Unfortunately, his life and our partnership in co-authoring this book was cut short on July 11, 2001, when another driver hit his car head-on near West Glacier, Montana. His free spirit and his legacy still roam the wild lands of the place he loved most, Glacier National Park. This one's for you Monty.

CONTENTS

PREFACE AND ACKNOWLEDGMENTS

Monty and I were relaxing on the beach at Saint Mary Lake one day in early July of 1993. It was too windy to fish. The tall cottonwoods behind us bent under the gales sweeping down the Saint Mary Valley. We watched mist waft off whitecaps. Large waves rolled past us on the pebbled shore. Just behind the cottonwoods lay the site of our home for so many summers, the Sun Camp Ranger Station. In disrepair after years of service, the old cabin had been torn down and its last vestiges removed. We listened as the leaves of nearby quaking aspen rattled in the powerful gusts. They seemed to whisper tales of treasured times now long past, times we'd shared in this pristine place.

From time to time, our eyes filled with tears as we reminisced. So many experiences from our childhood had their beginnings here. It was there on that windy afternoon that the concept of this book was born.

Time passed and later that fall, we began jotting down memorable highlights we felt deserved a place in this collection of stories. After Monty's untimely death in July, 2001, I vowed to carry on the work we'd begun. My keen desire was to relate the magic and the adventure woven through our many park experiences.

Without doubt, my beloved brother, Monty Parratt, was the inspiration that compelled me to finish this project. I regret that some of the stories he wished to tell were not committed to paper before his death. However, many of the accounts of our boyhood experiences involve his notes and his thoughts. One insightful story, *The Old Blister Rust Days,* was written by Monty.

Prior to her recent passing at age ninety-three, our mother, Grace Parratt, contributed invaluable information spanning the era from the late 1940's through the 1950's. My youngest brother, Smitty Parratt, is a very special contributor to this project. Kay Dell Parratt, my remarkable wife, has spent untold hours proofreading and editing as each story evolved. Without her love, support, and knowledge of the park, this book would never have come to be.

Russ Schneider deserves special thanks for his continual encouragement and editorial guidance. Carl and Patricia Rosenleaf provided valuable insights. In addition, the following individuals were of help: Kim Schneider, Laurel Parratt, Krissy Parratt, Ev and Margaret Lundgren, Jerry Bell, Ken and Marilyn Proctor, Viola Clark, Bob and Ann Frauson, Larry Dale, William Colony and Curt Buchholtz.

Although they are no longer with us, I feel I owe a great debt of gratitude to my legendary parents, Lloyd and Grace Parratt. In their memory, I will continue to savor the Glacier Park they taught us to know and love so well. Each time I hear the rustling of the wind through the aspen or the waves lapping the lakeshore, I will feel the spirits of my loved ones beside me.

Mark W. Parratt

Editors Note: Unless credited otherwise, all stories written by Mark Parratt.

Young Mark, Smitty and Monty with the early morning catch.

INTRODUCTION

From the shores of Saint Mary Lake to the top of Going-to-the-Sun Mountain.

Our father, Lloyd Parratt, was employed as a seasonal ranger naturalist in Glacier National Park during the summers from 1945 to 1963. With each June, we'd pack the family station wagon to overflowing and set out on the long trek from southern California to Glacier's mountain paradise.

We spent our first five summers in a rustic cabin nestled in the beautiful rain forest of Lake McDonald valley. As young boys, Monty and I eagerly learned the finer points of fishing under Dad's watchful eye. *Misadventures at Snyder Creek* shadows two small fishermen, toting willow poles, on a comical pursuit of the wily trout.

In the summer of 1951, Dad was transferred to the Saint Mary district on the park's east side. The isolated Sun Camp Ranger Station became our home for nine summer seasons to follow. Built in the 1930's, our log cabin nudged the shoreline at the northern edge of Saint Mary Lake. Sheltered by a grove of aged cottonwoods, we were serenaded by the rushing waters of nearby Baring Creek. The primitive cabin was accessible only by boat or trail.

Constant companions during those blissful summers, my brother Monty and I felt certain we were the luckiest boys on earth.

Our first season at Saint Mary, young brother Smitty was a baby in Mom's rucksack. Although too young to join us in many of our activities, a few years later, he is a central figure in *The Otokomi Grizzly Bear Attack*. An unfortunate victim in this heart-pounding tale of courage and survival, Smitty is well suited to co-author this story. The attack and its aftermath forever changed the lives of the entire Parratt family in a saga that continued for many years.

Arranged chronologically, the stories run from humorous tales in Glacier to life and death experiences in this wild and rugged place. The stories encompass everything from up close and personal grizzly bear attacks to dramatic search and rescue missions. With the angler in mind, I've included several memorable fishing tales. Finally, included are several gripping adventures drawn from my five summers as a park fireguard.

Fate Is A Mountain tells of a time and place very different from the Glacier Park of today. National Park Service policies and attitudes have changed considerably over the past decades.

So, come along with me to treasured times gone by, times of innocence and wonder, times of growth and awakening... times of truth and courage.

1

MISADVENTURES AT SNYDER CREEK

August 1950 - Mark and Monty Parratt - Lake McDonald

It was early August of 1950. I was nine and Monty, a very athletic six years of age. Without a doubt our passion was fishing. Throughout the summer, we'd managed to fish over thirty lakes, creeks and rivers on both sides of Glacier's Continental Divide. Either Dad or one of his fellow ranger naturalists always accompanied us when our outings took us beyond our home in the Lake McDonald valley.

As summer progressed, we could often be found at nearby Snyder Creek, fishing sections close to the main park road. Located only a few hundred yards from Beattyville, our park service cabin complex, the small stream was usually predictable for a good day's catch of small trout.

Earlier in the season, Dad had taken us on a steep four and a half mile hike to Lower Snyder Lake. We'd spent the day

National Park Service housing at Beattyville near Lake McDonald Lodge.

catching a host of small eastern brook and a few rainbows. Occasionally, a trout of twelve inches or more would take our bait.

This bolstered our hopes of someday fishing the upper reaches of Snyder Creek. The lake's only outlet, the small, tumbling watercourse rushed downhill to the place where it eventually spilled into Lake McDonald.

Our fishing poles were pliable six foot branches cut from alders or willows which grew near the family cabin. The setup we liked to use included a ten foot leader tied to the tip of the pole followed by a split shot sinker and a hook. Our bait was kindly provided by Smiley, a packer who helped run the nearby stables for the local concessionaire's horseback trips. The rich soil in the horse corrals produced large earthworms, perfect for our fishing adventures. Smiley considered himself well paid for his efforts each time Mom sent us over to his bunkhouse with a piece of her renowned huckleberry pie. In the manner taught by his father, Dad showed us how to keep the crawlers healthy in ventilated coffee cans filled with a mixture of soil and coffee grounds. Our mainstay, they were always ready at a moment's notice.

Young Monty Parratt continued his prowess as a fisherman, shown here at age thirteen with a fine string of trout.

We also discovered that the common grasshopper was irresistible to a hungry trout. On any given day near a roadside wedge of grasses, tourists watched curiously as two young boys crawled along on their hands and knees, occasionally pouncing on the hapless hoppers with cupped hands, but they were hard to catch and difficult to keep alive for more than a few days.

After weeks of anticipation, the sun finally dawned on our very own first all day fishing trip. Dad had given the two of us his approval to fish the remote upper reaches of Snyder Creek. Our excitement knew no bounds. After a hearty breakfast and last minute safety instructions from Mom, we eagerly readied our bait and fishing gear and we were out the door.

Passing through the filtered shade of the forest, we quickly lost sight of our family cabin. We picked up our pace as we crossed the park road and made our way to the Sperry Chalet trailhead. Roughly paralleling Snyder Creek, the fairly steep two mile climb eventually brought us to our destination where a bridge spanned the tumbling waters.

Excitement grew as we picked our way down the creek. Reaching the streambed at last, we nervously readied our poles. It wasn't long before we discovered fishing the creek here was hard work. We bushwhacked endlessly and picked our way over large downed trees and boulders. The wet rock beside the stream was covered with moss and algae, almost guaranteeing slips and falls. Typical for August, the creek's flow had diminished, but the cascading water fell into occasional deep pools where hungry trout lay in wait. Warily approaching, we used our short poles to wend our way along the brushy streambed. Our hands shook as we trembled with excitement.

Although we began each day's fishing using grasshoppers for bait, our meager supplies generally were depleted before long and worms became our only alternative. We found instant success at the creek that day. On many occasions, the pool's largest trout was first to hit the bait. A well timed tug set the hook and the battle was on. Since the leader was tied to the tip of the pole, the only way to land our catch was to quickly fling it over our heads onto the rocks behind us. Dropping our poles to the ground, we'd crash through the dense brush on hands and knees searching for our wriggling bounty. The fish often threw the hook, making it a challenge to grab the slippery creature before it flipped back into the stream and disappeared.

At one point, we made our way across large boulders in search of the next pool. Rain began to fall in a slow, steady drizzle. We scarcely noticed as our clothing was already soaked from wading in the stream. After all, we were fishing and at that moment in time, nothing else mattered.

Summoning all his boyish strength, Monty struggled to the top of a large boulder. Hailing me from his lofty perch, he suddenly slipped on the wet surface and skidded on his bottom into the deep pool below. I frantically scanned the foaming waters. Only his pole and creel eventually floated to the surface. I shouted his name several times. "Monty. Monty. Are you there?" I stood midstream, oblivious to the icy water that swirled about me. At last, to my relief, I heard a small voice, "I'm over here, Mark? Over here." There he sat, perched on a narrow shelf of rock beside a small waterfall. A natural towhead, his straight blond hair clung to his forehead in wet spikes.

I yelled back, "You O.K.?"

The broad smile on his face answered my question. With boyish good humor, he was quite obviously delighted by his sudden dunking. As we waded about to collect the floating creel and pole, his only concern came with the query, "We didn't lose any fish did we? Well, did we?"

"No, Monty, your fish are all here," I chuckled. Not trusting my math, one by one, he carefully cradled each of the trout in his small hands, recounting his precious catch. The majority of the fish we landed that day were seven to eight inches in length, but occasionally we'd hook a brookie which ran ten to twelve.

Grasping our gear, we continued to make our way down the creek, occasionally fishing the bigger pools. At times, the stream bank became so steep, it was impassible. Our only option was to climb over the large boulders upslope and then bushwhack back to the creek bed as we searched for pools further downstream. During one such diversion, I slipped off a moss covered windfall and tumbled into the bushes below. The scourge of Snyder Creek abruptly ended my fall. Devil's club, a common shrub, is covered with very fine, sharp spines that break off when contacted. The needles immediately pierced my clothing, finding tender skin. Small and difficult to locate, the painful spikes did nothing to make my stiff, wet jeans more comfortable.

Moments later, I lost my footing near the edge of the creek and then regained it, only to slip once more, this time landing with a splash. I glanced at Monty, hoping for a word of sympathy. Giggling uncontrollably, he tried again and again but couldn't speak. It wasn't long before I joined him. There we sat, side by side, convulsed with laughter, as the cold, swirling water swept past us.

Spent at last, we decided it was time for lunch. With boyish appetites, we wolfed down peanut butter and jelly sandwiches, apples, and a candy bar each. Next, we set about cleaning our mess of fish, a total of fifteen nice trout. Although drenched and covered with a motley mixture of dirt, moss and pine needles, we sat there smiling in the downpour, elated with our day's efforts. We'd each endured the insults of devil's club, stinging nettles and mosquito bites. However, if asked, both of us would tell you that it just didn't get much better than this.

Soon, it was mid-afternoon and the sky began to darken noticeably. We reluctantly decided it was time to draw our day's fishing to a close and head for home. Since our angling had taken us only about a mile downstream, we knew that we'd have to bushwhack upslope to find the trail. First, we needed to cross a wide patch of overgrown windfalls. Almost as soon as we began to clamber over the slippery logs, Monty lost his balance and disappeared. A loud crash brought out my brotherly concerns. I yelled, "Monty, Monty. You O.K.?" There was no response. Once again, I called out, "Are you O.K.?"

I scrambled to the point where I'd last seen him and peered downward into the hollow. From deep in the underbrush, his impish grin beamed up at me. Patches of wet moss clung to his face. Eager to redeem himself, he quipped, "It's O.K., the fish are fine." With all the tumbles and mishaps of the day, there was no doubt that our fish were top priority. Never mind youthful bruises and scrapes; they'd heal in time.

As we slowly made our way up the slope to the trail, fatigue from the day's efforts began to take its toll. A mere ten feet from the path, I brushed against a small hornet's nest while dragging my foot over a log. The angry insects boiled out of the shadows and the chase was on. I shouted, "Hornets...run, Monty, run!" He needed no further coaching. A heavy swarm of the darting, stinging creatures pursued us as we struggled to reach the trail. Multitudes of them seemed to appear

The Parratt Family recounts the day's adventures on the shores of Lake McDonald.

from nowhere and they were relentless. With our precious cargo bobbing along at our sides, we ran as fast as our weary legs would carry us. Time and time again, the insects found their mark, evoking sharp cries of pain, which mingled with our footfalls in the deep forest.

As we rounded a sharp bend in the steep trail, arms flailing to ward off the hornets, we spotted a small group of hikers coming toward us. In raspy, breathless voices, we shouted a warning, "Hornets! Run!"

Misinterpreting our muddled calls, we heard the lead hiker scream, "Bear! Run!" At that, they all turned as one, quickly disappearing in full retreat down the trail.

Eventually, we glanced back and realized we'd finally outrun the hornets. Our legs could carry us no further and, slowing the pace, we dropped to the ground, exhausted. Stings began to form painful welts on our arms and necks. As we lay there on the trail, gasping for breath, I rolled over to look at Monty. The broad smile that covered his face at that moment still lives in my memory today.

At last, we slowly got to our feet and headed down the trail once again. Quickening our pace, we made an earnest attempt to run down the small band of fleeing tourists. We never saw them again. Our best guess was they'd run the better part of a mile back to the park road where they probably decided to abandon their hiking efforts for the day.

The sun cast long shadows as two weary brothers finally approached the little cabin at the lake's edge. Mom smiled as we tumbled in the door, offering tall glasses of lemonade to her grubby, trail-worn sons. As she readied cold compresses for our stings, she looked us over, remarking, "Snyder Creek must have been quite an adventure today."

Monty responded, "It was neat, Mom. We didn't even run into any bears." We glanced at each other and began to giggle.

Mom nodded, adding, "You two must have had a bath in the creek and then rolled in the dirt." Our mother didn't miss much; she knew her young fishermen pretty well.

She whisked us off to the community showers and made certain that we changed into clean, dry clothes. Before long, Dad arrived home from his day's ranger naturalist duties and dinner was served.

For some reason, freshly caught trout tasted extra special that evening. On his way home, our father had picked up a quart of hand-packed Glacier Gold ice cream from the soda fountain at Lake McDonald Hotel. Without doubt, it was the perfect topping for Mom's fresh, warm huckleberry pie.

Leaning back in his chair and smiling, Dad commended us on our fine catch. Sagely noting our scratches and welts from the day's adventure, he warned, "You two need to be more careful out there.

There are a lot of hornet nests on the ground this time of year. Next time you fish the creek, don't try it in the rain; it's just too slick on those rocks and logs." As usual, Dad was right and we both nodded in agreement.

Four days later, warm sun filled the air with the scent of pine as we headed through the forest to pick up the trail to the Snyder Creek bridge. It was time to go fishing again and, somehow, we felt like old hands.

2

A FUNCTIONAL
FISHERMAN ONCE AGAIN

June 1951 – Sun Camp Ranger Station

It was the summer of 1951 and many a Glacier evening was spent fishing near our cabin on Saint Mary Lake. It wasn't unusual to see the Parratt boys knee deep in the icy waters near the Baring Creek outlet from shortly after dinner until 11:00 P.M.

Occasionally, Monty and I chose to accompany Dad to his illustrated evening talk at the Saint Mary dormitory. On nights when he gave his campfire programs at Rising Sun, we were often seen perched on the rustic log bench closest to the fire. Dad was a true professional in the interpretive arts and a favorite

Smitty and Monty Parratt fish from the dock at Sun Camp.

with park visitors. Needless to say, we were extremely proud of him as well.

After hiking a quarter of a mile from our cabin to a pullout along the Going-to-the-Sun Road, we piled into the dark green park service pickup Dad kept there. The fifteen to twenty minute drive took us to the site of one of his programs.

I am certain, if Monty were still alive and I could ask him, he would vividly recall one particularly memorable event which occurred on our return from Saint Mary one night. It was cold and stormy and, at one point, the rain was so intense, we were forced to pull over to the side of the road to wait for the downpour to stop. Lightning illuminated the entire valley and the thunder was deafening.

As the storm cell eventually passed to the east, we pulled back onto the road and continued our journey homeward. In the storm's aftermath, the temperature dropped noticeably. Dad switched on the heater and Monty decided to warm his hands under it. Contained in a metal housing, the truck's heater was located just under the dashboard. Suddenly, its whirring fan stopped with a jolt. At the same time, Monty let out a piercing scream. Alarmed, Dad immediately pulled off the road. With the aid of a flashlight, we quickly discovered that one of the heater's fan blades was deeply embedded in Monty's finger. Feeling no initial pain, his attempts at pulling free were futile. In the beam of our flashlight, we tried repeatedly to help him, but the captive finger simply would not budge. A pool of blood began to accumulate on the rubber mat below the fan.

Trapped there, poor Monty was bewildered and distraught. In desperation, Dad decided to remove the heater. After several minutes of prying, he was able to bend the unit downward for a better view. The bleeding continued as tears began to slide down Monty's cheeks.

In an effort to collect his thoughts, Dad leaned back in his seat. The expression he wore did nothing to reassure us. Then, in desperation, Monty gave one more tug. To our amazement, he pulled free. A brief moment of euphoria was quickly followed by dismay. We were shocked to see his middle finger hanging there, attached only by a shred of skin. Visions spun through our minds of Monty going through life minus a finger. Pulling the park service first aid kit from behind the seat, Dad tightly wrapped Monty's injured hand in gauze.

Warmed by a wool blanket, Monty laid his head in my lap. I held my brother close as pain overtook him. He moaned softly. The bandage quickly turned to crimson as the bleeding persisted. It was obvious that Monty needed professional medical help, and he needed it soon.

Dad slammed the truck into gear and quickly headed back to Saint Mary. The truck screeched to a halt in front of Saint Mary Lodge. A request was soon made over the public address system asking anyone with medical training to step forward. As luck would have it, an elderly veterinarian and his wife were enjoying a late supper in the lodge's dining room. Earlier that evening, they had attended Dad's evening program and recognized us immediately. The vet quickly arose from his table and came forward, offering to help.

It was nearly midnight when the veterinarian finished tending Monty's injury. Cleaning and packing his finger in sulfa powder, the kindly gent then covered the entire hand with a tight bandage. As we parted, he told Dad that Monty needed to be seen by a surgeon within the next twelve hours. He recommended a specialist in Columbia Falls.

Since Logan Pass was closed for the evening due to rockslides and light snowfall, we were compelled to wait until the next morning to seek medical care. The manager of the lodge offered us a room for the night at no charge. Finding a telephone, Dad was finally able to place a call to Mom. Worries had nearly overcome her as she waited there in our cabin, cradling her youngest son in the dim light of a kerosene lantern.

With arrangements to meet Mom and two-year old Smitty at Sun Point the following morning, we fell into bed totally exhausted. At daybreak, the three of us climbed into the truck and headed up Going-to-the-Sun Road. It was 5:30 A.M. when we pulled into the parking lot at Sun Point. A transfer was quickly made and, with her three sons packed into the old Plymouth station wagon, Mom headed over Logan Pass, driving some seventy miles to Columbia Falls.

We arrived at the office of Dr. Bennett just as his nurse was unlocking the front door. The physician examined Monty immediately and asked his nurse to prepare for surgery. After a hefty dose of local anesthesia, the surgeon cleansed the wound and began to carefully suture ligaments and larger blood vessels. After reattaching the finger, he added a splint and a thick dressing. We were told it would take several weeks for the severed finger to heal. It was anyone's guess as to how functional it would be in the long term. After injecting Monty with a small dose of morphine, he sent us on our way.

Young Monty after treatment for his injured finger.

With a sense of relief, we headed over the pass toward home. Monty slept most of the way and awakened just before we reached the trailhead to our cabin. I kept a tight grip on his left arm as we wended our way down the trail. Still groggy from the morphine, the little fellow persisted in wandering off into the bushes. As a last resort, I clung to his belt loop in an effort to keep the wounded adventurer headed toward the cabin.

Dr. Bennett had given Mom an ample supply of dressings as well as careful instructions for Monty's daily care. It wasn't surprising when my young brother had nightmares about the heater fan for several nights in a row.

Two weeks passed quickly and soon it was time to remove Monty's stitches. Fortunately, a nurse and her husband were stationed at the Reynolds Mountain Fire Lookout tower. Early one morning, Monty and I hiked the five miles up the Saint Mary valley to the lookout. The kind and caring woman there quickly removed the stitches and announced the finger was healing nicely. She reminded Monty to work the finger regularly to keep it from stiffening.

The strawberry Kool Aid she served us was the best we'd ever tasted. As evidence, the Parratt boys each managed to consume four large glasses before heading down the mountain.

Monty diligently exercised his finger and, slowly, sensation and mobility began to return. I recall how he beamed with pleasure as he reeled in his first trout since the accident, realizing he was a functional fisherman once again. Later, Monty remarked how the scar on his finger would always serve as a reminder of a frightening experience on a very stormy Glacier night.

3
SQUATTER'S RIGHTS

August 1951 – Sun Camp Ranger Station

Grace Parratt would have made a wonderful pioneer woman. Strong-willed and intelligent, she had to rely on her best instincts during the many summers our family spent living in the primitive Sun Camp Ranger Station. Surrounded by trails leading to the park road, our isolated cabin provided unique challenges to a wife, homemaker and mother of three. One morning, Dad set off for work, forgetting his lunch. No problem. Mom finished up her morning chores and resolved to deliver his noon meal on foot. As a park service ranger naturalist, Dad's duties that day involved fielding questions at the Sun Point information station. The small, one-room hut was encircled by windows which commanded a stunning view of Saint Mary Lake and the station was a mere one-mile trek from the cabin.

With one-year old son, Smitty, tucked into a baby carrier on her back and lunch in hand, Mother Parratt ventured forth. As she closed the cabin door and turned toward the trail, she was immediately confronted by a large black bear. The shaggy beast emitted a series of loud woofs, as

Grace Parratt carries Smitty
to
Sun Camp Ranger Station.

it aggressively moved toward her. Keeping an eye on the bear, Mom stopped abruptly, backed up slowly, and slipped back into the cabin.

From within, she could hear the bear brushing against the door, then slowly circling the structure. Standing on its hind legs, the bruin peered into windows and pawed the logs, obviously intent on gaining entry. Alone in the cabin with her young son, she was genuinely frightened. Yet, with her typical resolve, she was still intent on delivering Dad's lunch and she wasn't about to let a bear deter her.

A half hour passed as she listened to the animal prowling around outside the cabin. At last, the bear discovered the end of the drain pipe leading from the kitchen sink. Bits of the morning's breakfast deposited there proved irresistible to the hungry critter. He poked, prodded and slurped at the murky puddle for several minutes. Watching the scene from her kitchen window, Mom waited patiently.

Slowly, another half hour passed. Uneasy at first, now she became genuinely irritated. Her husband's lunch was long overdue. Suddenly, in desperation, instinct took over. Grasping a container of

Sun Camp Ranger Station on Saint Mary Lake.

liquid bleach, she quickly poured about a cup down the kitchen sink and turned on the faucet. Moments later, the potent solution reached the end of the drain pipe. The dining bruin suddenly let out a loud belch and then tumbled over backwards. Pawing at his nose, he let out several yelps. Struggling to his feet, the bear turned and galloped down the trail which led away from the cabin, disappearing over a hill nearby.

Shortly after the bruin's sudden departure, Mom, once again let herself out of the cabin. This time, she made an uneventful trek ending with the successful delivery of dad's lunch.

The same bear, with an unmistakable blond patch on his rump, was seen two days later at nearby Rising Sun Campground turning over trash cans. Within another week, the hapless bruin was live trapped and moved to a remote section of Glacier Park.

4
MOOSE BUTT

June 1952 - Mark and Monty Parratt — Sun Camp Ranger Station

I remember the summer of 1952 with great fondness. Dad had signed on for another summer working as a seasonal ranger naturalist for the National Park Service. Set near the beachfront on upper Saint Mary Lake, the remote Sun Camp Ranger Station would again be our home for the next three months.

I was eleven and Monty, my brother and fellow adventurer, was three years my junior. We hiked, fished, climbed and explored almost every day that we weren't helping Mom with chores.

One August morning, we'd caught several mountain whitefish at a point where Baring Creek spills into the lake, mere feet from our front door. We crouched there at the water's edge cleaning and scaling our beautiful catch. Then, bearing the fish up to the cabin,

Fishing off the dock at Sun Camp Ranger Station.

we gladly accepted smiling accolades from our young mother. All three agreed, fish and fried spuds would make a fine evening meal.

As lunchtime approached, we fell into the boyhood pattern of gentle teasing and chasing one another about. On this particular occasion, Monty climbed part way up a nearby fir tree and then shinnied to the ground. Grinning devilishly, he approached me, pine pitch covering the palms of his hands. As I darted to avoid him, he gleefully set about chasing me, sticky hands thrust out in front of him. Naturally, my reaction was, "No way. I don't want that stuff all over me." I fled. Glancing back, I realized that he was gaining on me. The only way I could avoid the prankster was to head up the trail that led away from the cabin.

Casting another quick glance behind me, I noted with satisfaction that I was distancing myself from the scamp. Intent on my escape, I congratulated myself, "Aha. I showed him!"

Running as fast as I could, I turned to face the trail once again. Nothing could have prepared me for what happened next. Without warning, I blindly propelled myself into a very large, immovable object in the middle of the trail. Thrown off-balance by the sudden collision, my body ricocheted off the obstacle and met the trail with a resounding thud. Stunned, I lay there for a moment. As my mind slowly cleared, my eyes came to focus on a huge, hairy animal. Sorting out the details, I realized I had run headlong into the rear end of a large bull moose who clearly had the right of way on the trail.

Slowly turning his massive head, he gazed back at me as if to say, "Now, what was that all about?" Then, with no further ado, the ungainly animal slowly ambled down the path as though nothing had happened. Sitting there in the middle of the trail, I breathed a fervent sigh of relief, then stood up and dusted myself off.

Monty was a nearby witness to the unexpected collision. Fearful of what might happen next, he sped back to the cabin to alert Mom. In typical boyhood fashion, he blurted out, "Mom! Mom! Mark was just attacked by a horrible big beast." Suspecting the worst, she came running to my aid just in time to see the shaggy brown moose lumber out of sight around a bend in the trail.

She quickly examined me and determined that I was unharmed other than the large, red welt which stood out on my forehead. Puzzled by the situation, she asked me to describe what had happened. Now, realizing the danger to which I had unwittingly exposed myself, I cried, "Mom! Monty was chasing me with pine pitch all over his hands. I wasn't looking where I was going and I ran right into the back end of that moose."

Monty joined us on the trail as her laughter bubbled forth. Soon she was unable to stop and every now and then she would gasp, "I don't believe it. I just don't believe it." Finally she added, "Now, Mark, that is really some story. Wait 'til your dad hears about this one." Taking my hand, she led me slowly back down the trail to the cool confines of the cabin for lunch and a cold compress for my head. I still recall my distinct embarrassment, as the entire family persisted in repeating the moose-crash story to all who would listen over the days to come.

Upon hearing the unlikely tale, Dad simply patted me on the shoulder and commented, "Mark, that was truly an up close and personal visit with a moose. I'm sure glad you're O.K., son. However, next time it might be wise to look where you're going."

5

FISH THIEF

At last, Monty and I had truly discovered the mother lode of fishing. It was a particularly hot afternoon in mid July of 1952. Lying within the dense forested valley formed by Citadel Peak and Reynolds Mountain is a formidable section of shrub-covered country dotted with swamps, ponds and beaver dams. The Saint Mary River courses its way through these wetlands, fed by numerous tributaries running off the nearby mountain slopes.

We'd spent several days exploring both sides of the river from Saint Mary Falls into the upper Saint Mary Valley almost to Gunsight Lake. We had found little fishing success so far, with only an occasional small trout here and there. Trudging through mud, we were surrounded by dense alder and willow thickets. As was often the case, we were wading chest-deep in cold water. A black swarm of mosquitoes followed our every move. We felt certain that no modern man had either the patience or the fortitude to really fish the area thoroughly; it was simply too rugged and time consuming.

Sweaty and tired after a morning of crisscrossing another section of backwater, we sat on a downed tree near the water's edge. I glanced at my brother and said, "Why don't we just hike on up to Gunsight Lake and bring home a mess of smaller fish? We've had good luck there before. Besides, I just don't think we'll find any fish here…I really don't."

Smiling, Monty looked up at me and said, "Ah…Let's give it a chance. I know there's something here…I can just feel it."

Less than enthusiastic after spending so much time exploring the soggy basins, I munched on my peanut butter sandwich and finally murmured, "O.K. then, if you say so. Let's check out those little ponds up there." I nodded toward a series of beaver dams we'd bypassed earlier that day. "If we don't find some good fishing, let's head back to the cabin and do something different tomorrow."

I was eleven and Monty, age eight. We were perfectly matched, constant companions who loved spending those long boyhood summer days exploring the Saint Mary Valley. Weather permitting, most of our waking hours found us immersed in fishing, boating, hiking, climbing, or just exploring.

We pushed our way through the brush and finally found a clearing on higher ground where we could see a series of at least seven beaver dams, strung together, wending their way up the valley. With nervous excitement, we assembled our rods and prepared to test the waters in the first pond. The dam that created it was massive, made up of branches of all sizes packed together tightly with mud to back up the slow moving water. A trickle cascaded over the end of the dam. Near one side of the pond stood a largely submerged beaver hut.

The bait of choice for such an occasion was the grasshopper. A few days earlier, we'd spent hours on our hands and knees catching a few dozen of these hopping denizens of the grasslands. We'd discovered that a hungry trout simply couldn't resist a grasshopper on a size-eight hook. Placing a few small split shot sinkers a few feet above the bait, I nervously cast the first line some ten feet into the pool as Monty watched. Crouching behind the willows, we waited patiently. My bobber floated on the placid surface with no movement. Nothing. We both fished the pond for several minutes without a single nibble. A few minnows could be seen tracking the depths, but no activity was discernable. Satisfied this was yet another fishing dud, we moved up to the next pond. Over a period of an hour, we fished five of the pools. Monty caught two small rainbows and released them.

The sixth pond in the series was much larger than the others. It appeared to have an undercut bank on one side and stretched in a long, narrow band for at least fifty yards or so. We silently crept up to the far end and began casting our rigs. I'd just baited a fresh grasshopper, when Monty's pole bent double. "Mark, this one's a monster! Get the net. Get the net ready." After a ten minute wrestle with the spinning, flashing trout, he slowly brought his catch toward the water's edge. I plunged the net into the churning surface and finally managed to snare the fish on my third attempt.

Monty proudly eyed the good-sized trout with the biggest smile and said, "See what I mean?" The *de Liar* weighing device proved the trout to be just over four pounds and seventeen inches in length. We were thrilled, but, with the enthusiasm of youth, were eager to see if the pond would yield a second nice fish.

Only moments later, I hooked another nice one. Though it put up a beautiful fight, Monty finally secured the trout in the net. The fish was just a tick under four pounds.

By now, we were really excited. This made the last seven days of bushwhacking, mud and mosquitoes all worthwhile. Satisfied with our respective catches, we were ready to leave when Monty insisted on one last cast.

Within minutes, he'd hooked another good-sized fish that put up a vigorous fight. The fish had dragged out some twenty feet of line before it flashed near the surface. Now in the center of the pond, the frantic creature continued to dive to the bottom, then spiral to the surface with a loud splash.

Suddenly, out of the corner of my eye, I caught the rapid movement of a dark object plummeting downward into the pond. With incredible speed and agility, a large bird splashed the surface of the water just as the struggling trout appeared once again. With unbelievable dexterity, the bird quickly lifted the fish up and away. Grasping its prey, it silently disappeared into the forest canopy.

The fishing line sprung back smartly as the bird hit the fish. With a sharp twang, the hapless leader flipped into the top of the tallest willow behind us. Monty shouted, "Did you see that? What was it?" I suspected some type of fish hawk, but we'd have to ask Dad, our resident bird expert.

After numerous attempts, Monty finally gave up trying to untangle his fishing line. His entire rig, including the bare hook was hopelessly wrapped around the stout mass of vegetation. He broke off the leader, retrieving the remainder of his line. We packed our gear into rucksacks and made our way out of the marsh.

Caught up in the excitement of the afternoon, we trekked to the nearby Saint Mary River and dressed out our fish. Two happier lads could not be found in Glacier National Park as we bushwhacked back to the main trail that afternoon and headed home.

After listening to our story, Dad said he felt certain that a Goshawk (fish hawk) was the culprit in the remarkable fish theft saga. He stressed that we had witnessed a marvel of nature far more unique than catching two nice trout. We couldn't help but nod in agreement. That night, as we whispered back and forth from our bunks, we were in total agreement that catching big fish in beaver ponds was, indeed, a very special experience. We returned to the pond several times during the following summers and always caught a few two to three-pound trout. In a boyhood pact, we made it our secret spot, and we never divulged its location to anyone.

Sadly, nature took its toll on the beaver pond fishing in the mid-sixties with an early summer flood that hit the park with a vengeance. The entire wetlands area was wiped out by rising floodwaters from the Saint Mary River. We returned the following summer to find no evidence of beaver activity. Only boulders and piles of debris left by the restless waters marked the sacred spot that we'd cherished.

On a fishing trip to Glacier in August, 1984, we discovered several new beaver ponds in the recovering backwaters. We caught and released a number of five to six-inch trout in two different ponds. This time it was a mix of cutthroat and rainbow trout. Since that time, we've not returned to fish the ponds, but suspect strongly that a good many of those small trout could, indeed, be the big ones by now.

6

ST. ELMO'S FIRE

August 1952 – Curly Bear Fire Lookout

A cloud of thick white dust ebbed past the park service pickup. The long bumpy ride had brought us, at last, to the end of Red Eagle truck trail. Ellen and I hesitated a moment for the air to clear, then slid from the cab. Bidding farewell to the driver, we shrugged into our backpacks and approached the nearby trailhead. Our objective for the morning was a sentinel which stood far above the forested valley, the Curly Bear Fire Lookout.

Ellen Counts and her husband, Ed, were hired by the park service to manage the lookout during Glacier Park's summer fire season. Scattered throughout the park's two-million acres were a number of these strategically located towers. Young married

Forest fire has always been a natural part of Glacier's ecosystem, but fire-fighting philosophy has changed markedly over the years.

couples were often chosen to man the remote mountain outposts. With such an arrangement, if one of the pair wished to hike out for a day or so, the spouse could remain at the tower on fire watch.

The Counts had become close friends with my parents over the past several seasons. Ed heard of my fascination with fire lookout towers and suggested that I might wish to spend a night with them at Curly Bear. I had visited several towers on day hikes over the past few summers, but had yet to spend the night at one.

In order to rendezvous, Ellen would hike out to the trailhead where Dad would pick her up, and bring her to spend the night with us at Sun Camp Ranger Station. The next morning, he would take the two of us back to the trailhead. Together, Ellen and I would hike the three-plus miles to the lookout. Dad assured me the experience was sure to be a thrill any youngster would envy. At eleven, little did I suspect the impact the upcoming adventure would have on my life in summers to follow.

As the morning progressed, we made our way up the trail. It became noticeably cooler as we traversed the countless switchbacks through patches of alder and broken evergreen forest. The final mile included an elevation gain of over eighteen-hundred feet. Buffeted by strong winds, we paused to rest several times on the steep trail. At last, warning chirps of marmots and pikas signaled our arrival atop the alpine ridge.

There it was, resting just a few hundred feet ahead. The majestic structure seemed somehow out of place on the stark, rocky pinnacle.

Leaning on the deck's railing, Ed watched us as we slowly approached on the narrow pathway below. The thin alpine air had taxed our strength during the steep climb and the tower before us was a welcome sight, indeed. Ed shouted, "You must have made pretty good time on the way up. Welcome to our window on the world." We slowly worked our way to the top of the steep wooden stairway. Ed held his wife at arm's length, and then, affectionately embraced her.

He glanced toward me and with a playful grin, asking "Now, who is your young friend, Ellen?" For a fleeting moment, I felt like an intruder. I cast a curious glance at Ellen, and we all burst into laughter. Ed shook my hand and then hefted the pack from my shoulders. He queried, "So, I guess you've never spent a night in a fire lookout tower?" I shook my head. "We're glad you're here, Mark. I'll bet you're both ready for some lunch." Feeling a bit overwhelmed, I nodded shyly and was ushered into the airy tower.

The Curly Bear Fire Lookout was a room fourteen feet square that loomed some twelve feet above a rocky base. The flooring was supported by massive wooden beams. Heavy braided steel cables further anchored each corner, providing stability in the gale force winds that frequently blasted the tower. An outer catwalk completely encircled the building. Inside the sunlit room, large windows provided a stunning 360-degree vista of the mountain slopes below.

The middle of the room was dominated by the *Osborne Fire Finder*. The device, supported by a central post, displayed a circular park map placed near eye level. Crosshairs were used to pinpoint precise coordinates for fire sightings. Readings radioed from these calibrations enabled ground fire crews armed with a compass and a topographic map to locate even the smallest blaze in heavy timber.

A large wood stove, table and chairs, three metal spring beds, a couple of dressers and a cupboard comprised the remainder of the room's modest furnishings. Coleman lanterns provided light for the evening hours. A rustic outhouse was reached by a short trail leading from the base of the lookout.

Ed had prepared peanut butter and jelly sandwiches. Paired with tall glasses of ice cold Kool Aid, they really hit the spot. Later, helping with the chores, I discovered the lookout's fresh water was carried by hand from a nearby spring. Here, it was drawn and hauled to the tower, where it was stored in five gallon Jeep cans.

As we ate our lunch, I gazed out upon the beautiful panorama far below us. Ellen remarked, "It doesn't get much better than this." I smiled in agreement.

The Canadian Rocky Mountains could be seen stretching one-hundred miles to the north. To the west loomed the beautiful U-shaped Saint Mary valley with towering peaks rising on both sides. The far end of the valley was punctuated by the jagged skyline of the Continental Divide.

By late afternoon, I noted a large, ominous storm front moving down the valley in our direction. Sitting down for dinner, we glanced up to see flashes of lightning in the distance. As the storm quickened its advance, our meal came to an abrupt halt. My hosts quickly arose from the table and, without hesitation, launched into a full scale fire watch.

July had been unusually hot and Glacier's forests were now tinder dry. Not surprisingly, the Smoky Bear signs throughout the park had warned of extreme fire danger for weeks.

"Good heavens," Ellen exclaimed, "I can't believe the number of lightning strikes out there. Mark, I think we're in for a real electrical display tonight." I watched in awe as the young woman skillfully pinpointed and then recorded each hit with the fire finder.

Meanwhile, Ed continually searched the horizon with a powerful binocular. He murmured, "Headquarters was dead right about this storm. It could get nasty."

"Nasty," I thought. "Maybe this overnight thing wasn't such a good idea after all."

The large, battery powered radio began to crackle as the lookout crew on distant Reynolds Mountain called park headquarters to report the locations of lightning strikes which now stabbed nearby mountaintops and ridges. Their broadcast was broken up by the loud cracking sound of static interference. Ed explained, "Every one of those cracks is a lightning strike near their lookout. By the sound of it, they're really getting bombarded right now. Lightning is certainly a tremendous force of nature." I could feel the excitement mounting as the fierce storm moved still closer.

Then, far below us, a particularly large lightning bolt struck near Red Eagle Lake. Moments later, we observed a faint wisp of smoke curling upward from the site of the strike. Ed quickly positioned the fire finder and called the smoke in to park headquarters. Musing for a moment, he declared, "Sure hope they received that message. With all this damn static, I really can't tell. Once this moves past us, I'll give 'em another try." Piercing the flanks of nearby mountains, the brilliant flashes became brighter as they approached. Next, a strike near the summit of East Flattop Mountain caught Ed's attention as it emitted an eerie glow.

Ellen gasped, "This is amazing."

Booming thunder now rattled the large glass windowpanes. The smoke of the distant fires faded as clouds and driving rain charged up the slope toward us.

Suddenly, a large lightning bolt struck the rocks some 500 feet below us. Following the strike, a brilliant halo of light appeared briefly above the outcrop. "Look, Mark. That's what they call *Saint Elmo's Fire.*" I could sense genuine excitement in Helen's voice. She explained that the phenomenon sometimes occurs when a static electric charge glows for several seconds above a strike. It was exciting to witness the bizarre event which I'd heard occasionally discussed in the company of mountain climbers.

Now, with brilliant flashes all about, Ed was quick to warn us not to touch metal objects in the room. For emphasis, he placed a hand on each of my shoulders and looked squarely into my eyes, commanding, "Mark. Don't touch anything made of metal during this storm. People have been killed that way." His order registered as I quickly moved away from the bed and seated myself warily on a small wooden chair near the center of the room. Little did I realize, at the time, I would spend the rest of the night clinging there.

Within moments of its approach, the main front of the electrical storm moved directly above us. Strikes hitting the tower were drawn to the lightning rod near the outside railing. Hearing a violent crack, I jerked my head around to see a bright white electrical charge move quickly down the grounding cable, disappearing through a small hole in the floor. A portion of each charge occasionally glowed as it passed through the cable which ran to the beds and other metal furnishings in the room. As the strikes continued in rapid staccato, my heart began to pound. Multiple arcs flashed on all sides. A blinding flash of light and the sound of simultaneous deafening thunder meant the lightning had scored a direct hit on the building. Several such hits occurred in rapid succession. Ed shouted above the clamor, "In all our summers here, we've never seen lightning like this."

There's no place like a fire lookout in a lightning storm.

From my youthful perspective at the time, I felt certain the tower was either going to explode or catch fire at any moment. The thick, sour odor of ozone generated by the lightning now filled the room. For the next half hour, we witnessed a continuous light show as brilliant flashes illuminated the dimly lit space. All efforts at conversation were abandoned. At last, the mêleé reached such intensity that a chair bounced across the floor toward the opposite side of the room. I watched in amazement as a cabinet rattled open, sending a cascade of pots and pans tumbling out and skidding about the floor.

Terrified, I reached out and clutched Ellen's hand. A tingling electrical charge suddenly passed between us. Glancing at her, I was stunned to see her long red hair standing straight up from her head. Seeing my shocked expression, she reassured me that static electricity surrounding us was responsible for her strange appearance. If I hadn't been so frightened at the time, the scene would have been hilarious.

As the fierce lightning finally moved past Curly Bear Mountain, the tower was engulfed in swirling clouds. Then came a barrage of rain that continued for hours. Howling winds pushed sheets of water in surges which blasted the large windows relentlessly and buffeted the spindly tower. With each gust, the entire structure creaked and shuddered.

At last, during the early morning hours, the storm finally spent its fury and moved on. I felt a genuine sense of relief as the darkness slowly ebbed into daylight. Sunrise was born with a soft, orange glow that gradually bathed the surrounding peaks. Reassuringly, Ellen patted me on the shoulder and declared, "See, we're all okay."

Not wishing to bare my soul, I murmured, "Yeah, that was really neat." Meanwhile, I was thinking to myself, "I can't believe we're all still alive. I can't get off this mountain soon enough." I reflected how the calm, beautiful morning was such a sharp contrast to the long, turbulent night.

With the storm system now past, forest fires throughout the park became top priority. The locations of the previous night's lightning strikes were, once again, carefully checked using the fire finder. In spite of the intense rainfall, two fires reported the previous evening were still active. Ed noted that large bolts of lightning can generate temperatures of 50,000 degrees Fahrenheit, easily igniting a wet snag or a live tree. Other blazes could be sleepers that smoldered, unnoticed, for weeks before popping up as a smoke plume.

One fire's location was marked at about 500 feet above the base of Red Eagle Lake. The blaze was putting up a dense column of smoke that would make it easy to spot for the approaching ground crew.

On the flank of East Flattop Mountain, another fire continued to smolder in a tree snag, emitting small, intermittent wisps of smoke. A crew was being dispatched to this fire as well. Ed noted, "You know those darn snags can smolder for hours or, sometimes, days before they show smoke or flames. Once those babies flare up, they can break apart and tumble down the mountainside. I saw that happen, once, down in the Payette National Forest in Idaho. Those falling embers started a bunch of small fires in no time. One of them burned thousands of acres and crews worked for three weeks to put the darned thing out."

As the morning wore on, fire lookouts on both sides of the Continental Divide reported several small blazes. It would be a busy day for the fire crews throughout the park. A spotter plane was dispatched to fly over remote areas. The radio was alive with chatter as the dispatcher from park headquarters busily coordinated the fire suppression efforts.

Suddenly, in the midst of all this, I felt an overwhelming desire to be with my family.

A brief breakfast brought us to my time of departure. I said goodbye and thanked my hosts. Down at the base of the stairs, I gave the tower one last respectful glance, waved, then turned and quickly started down the pathway toward the switchbacks. Once lost from view of the lookout, my pace quickened and I broke into a run. Somehow, distancing myself from the events of the previous night produced a calming effect. The steep twists and turns in the trail seemed to flow past me as my feet pounded the narrow path.

Curiously, at that moment, I somehow knew that, one day, I, too, wanted to be a firefighter with the park service. Manning a fire tower seemed lonely and confining. My choice, I decided, would be to work amongst the action and excitement which took place with fire crews.

I rounded the last bend in the trail and my spirits soared as I spotted Dad and my brother, Monty, in a waiting pickup truck. Embracing Dad in a hug, I blurted, "Dad, you won't believe what we saw last night at the lookout. It was so scary. I was sure I was going to die."

Dad chuckled and replied, "I'll bet it was frightening. Why don't you tell us about it?" My harrowing tale of the incredible night atop Curly Bear spilled out in lively conversation during the bumpy ride out of the backcountry.

Finally, Dad interrupted my chatter and tapped me on the shoulder. Laughing, he chided, "Easy now, big guy. Let's save some of the story for your mother."

It was heartwarming to return to the safety and comfort of our cabin at Sun Camp. Nestled amongst the cottonwoods on the shores of Saint Mary Lake, it was a peaceful haven for our family. As I lay in my cot that night, the hypnotic sounds of nearby Baring

Creek quickly lulled me to sleep.

Seven summers later, I realized my boyhood dream. I was hired as a fireguard in Glacier National Park. Stationed at the remote Belly River Ranger Station near the Canadian border, I became part of the park's firefighting force. Fire-guarding over the next five summers, I worked at various stations on the park's east side. Summers to follow would find me in California, where I led fire crews and coordinated air tanker drops in the Sierra Nevada's Toiyabe National Forest.

The acrid smell of a forest fire, the adrenaline rush, the excitement and camaraderie, still stoke my senses to this day. I will always hold in fond memory those adventure-filled summers inspired by that unforgettable night high on Curly Bear Mountain.

During the 1960's and 1970's, the majority of the park's network of fire lookout towers including those on Curly Bear and Reynolds Mountains were deemed obsolete and subsequently removed. Curly Bear Mountain Fire Lookout was razed and burned during the winter of 1964-65 by Saint Mary rangers, perhaps a fitting end to the enduring structure. At this time, a unique and very special part of Glacier's history lives on only in memory. Today, only a handful of the towers are still in existence and even fewer are still in use.

Meanwhile, fire spotter planes, helicopters and rapid response fire crews have modernized fire detection and suppression in the park. Changing scientific perspectives have also altered the perception of good fires vs. bad fires. Fire is now considered a vital and natural event through which the forest ecosystems are regenerated. As such, many fires that would have been suppressed in past decades are now carefully monitored and allowed to burn, providing positive benefits to Glacier's remarkable landscape.

During the summer of 2006, a human-caused fire began at the upper end of Red Eagle Lake. The ensuing fire storm and subsequent burn activity over a period of weeks incinerated much of the Red Eagle Valley and the Red Eagle Creek drainage. The path of the fire also consumed thousands of acres next to the shores of Saint Mary Lake. A concerted effort by firefighters managed to save the now-historic Saint Mary Ranger Station and surrounding park buildings.

The fire also burned up the slopes of our beloved Curly Bear Mountain, torching much of the forested area described in this story. The fire continued across a wide section of Highway 89 onto the Blackfeet Reservation where it burned out vast sections of forested land.

7

NIGHT QUILL

Our family arrived in Glacier Park for our summer-long stay in mid-June, 1953. We'd driven over Logan Pass on the Continental Divide as a light snow accumulated at the roadside. The Saint Mary valley and its majestic peaks were shrouded in clouds that hung low over the forested slopes. Old timers often referred to this weather condition as being socked in. The forecast called for continued fog, low clouds and cold rain. Typical weather this time of year, these dreary conditions often lasted for several days, sometimes weeks at a time.

The Parratt family, Mom, Dad and the three boys, labored for ten straight hours that day. Upon arrival, Dad parked our Plymouth station wagon in the large parking lot near the Sun Point information station. Bearing our worldly goods to the Sun Point boat dock, we loaded our canoe with large quantities of food and gear. Next, we paddled the choppy, gray lake for an hour just to reach our cabin. Totally exhausted by nightfall, we could feel the effects of six round trips with the canoe.

Returning as a park service ranger naturalist for his seventh summer, Dad was free from his official work duties for the next five days. With the inclement weather, at first, we were content to rest and set up the cabin for daily living. After our fourth day inside, however, we were beset with a serious case of cabin fever. Cold, wet weather or not, we were all eager for a change. Dad decided that a trip into the small town of Saint Mary would lift our spirits. Choosing not to brave the wind-whipped Saint Mary Lake in our canoe, we grabbed our rucksacks and ventured up the mile of trail that led to our parked car.

As we topped the trailhead and headed across the Sun Point parking area, Dad sensed that something was amiss. There sat our station wagon, resting unusually low on its wheel rims. A closer look revealed that all four tires were flat. Peering in disbelief, we discovered a large hole had been chewed in each of the new Goodyears. The gnaw marks closely resembled those found on small trees downed by beaver. Just then, a large porcupine scooted out from under the car and slowly ambled across the parking lot and into the forest. Dumbfounded, we looked in disgust at our disabled ride. Rubbing his chin, Dad asked, "How could a porcupine gnaw through steel-belted tires?"

Porcupines gnawed holes in the sidewalls of all four tires. This photo provided evidence for the insurance company.

The four-day trip from California had been trying enough. We'd endured six flat tires, mostly on the lengthy sections of endless road construction which dogged U.S. Highway 93 through Nevada, Idaho and Montana. Concerned for the safety of his family, Dad had decided to purchase four new tires in Missoula, a mere 150 miles from the car's final destination. Now here they were, totally destroyed.

They were in place and, indeed, had brought us to our destination.

Dejected, he crossed the wide parking lot to the Sun Point information station, where he used the primitive phone to call park headquarters. After the peculiar predicament was discussed, a workman from a tire company in Columbia Falls arranged to meet him in the parking lot the next day where the four ruined tires would be replaced.

Dad's final headache was attempting to collect a reimbursement from the auto insurance company in California. In a terse written response denying his claim they noted that, "We do not cover road hazards and our experts know of no claims that have ever been filed due to porcupine damage. Furthermore, it is not possible for such an animal to gnaw through steel-belted tires." Not to be outdone, Dad was equal to the challenge. He fired back letters written in his behalf from a park service biologist, the Chief Park Naturalist and a notarized affidavit confirming his story. Four months later, the insurance company did reimburse Dad for the tires.

A consensus of the park experts noted unusually large populations of yellow-haired porcupines in and around Glacier Park that year. They further emphasized that the salts used in the manufacture of synthetic rubber undoubtedly appealed to the porcupine's appetite, which led to the destruction of the tires. They guessed that the large rodents probably received quite a surprise when the tires blew out in their faces.

8

A QUESTIONABLE WATER SUPPLY

July 1953 - Mark and Monty Parratt — Sun Camp Ranger Station

A howling wind and driving rain dogged us as we struggled down the steep, muddy trail to Sun Camp Ranger Station. Our home for the summer, the rustic cabin there on the lakeshore was a stark contrast to our lifestyle in southern California. In a marathon that lasted four days, we made countless trips down to the cabin site from our station wagon at Baring Creek bridge. We carried in our belongings plus a three week food supply in rucksacks on our backs. Settled in our summer home at last, we'd earned a few days' rest before Dad officially began his job as a seasonal park ranger naturalist.

One of the rituals that marked the beginning of each summer was the appearance of park plumber, Elmer Senne. A colorful character, Elmer showed up like clockwork, a few days after our arrival. Bearing the tools of his trade in a leather rucksack, he set out to connect the cabin's unique water system. It took plenty of coffee and several of Mom's chocolate chip cookies before the park veteran built up enough energy to tackle the day long process.

Donning his hip boots, Elmer waded out into the creek and opened the underground water line which ran from the base of Baring Falls to the cabin. Soon, the glacial waters flowed through the taps and began filling the water heater attached to our large, wood-burning cook stove.

Elmer then examined the route of the underground water line from the intake to the cabin. More often that not, the winter freeze created leaks in the line that shot up out of the ground like small geysers. It took Elmer the remainder of the day to repair the leaks. In celebration of his success, Mom brewed up one of his favorite spaghetti dinners. As our honored guest, Elmer always enjoyed the hearty meal. Afterwards, we all sat around the table, entertained by his salty plumber stories.

A reality which inevitably struck us during the first week of each summer was a three to four day session of the Glacier quick-step, less delicately known as diarrhea. The glacial silt and a host of microbes in our water were the most likely culprits. Since our water

Baring Falls provided the Parratt family
with a constant supply of fresh water.

supply was not chlorinated, the difficulties we experienced came as no surprise. However, once the symptoms passed, we enjoyed the water the remainder of the summer without further problems.

One particular morning in late July, the wind roared down Saint Mary Valley like a runaway freight train. Fishing, much less standing erect, was out of the question, so Monty and I decided to do a bit of exploring. We had yet to follow Baring Creek from the top of the falls up to Sunrift Gorge, a distance of a quarter mile or so. We abandoned our fishing gear, packed a lunch and headed for Baring Falls. Climbing over a number of small cliffs and several downed trees, we gradually made our way up the creek.

A patch of huckleberries temporarily brought us to a halt. Large and purple, the tart berries were a delicious treat. Hefty swigs of water from the creek topped off our snack. We continued to brush beat and before long, the afternoon sun blazed down upon the creek bed. Here, sheltered from the relentless winds, we sat down on a patch of bear grass to enjoy our lunch.

As a warm breeze wafted past us, Monty suddenly sat bolt upright and blurted, "What is that horrible smell?" All too soon, I realized what he meant as the odor surrounded me in a putrid cloud. I quickly stuffed my sandwich into my backpack. Monty followed suit. Our appetites had vanished, overcome with the stench that brought to mind week-old road kill. I gasped, "Oh man. This is awful."

Determined to find the source of the odor, we slowly made our way upstream. As we climbed over a good sized boulder, Monty drew my attention to a strange sight ahead. There, in the middle of the creek was a black, hairy object wedged in a log jam. We couldn't help but notice that the odor became worse as we approached. Pinching our noses, we stared in disbelief as the bloated animal bobbed amongst the logs. Upon closer examination, we realized that the creature was a black bear. Appearing to be partially eaten, its green entrails flowed in rhythm with the current of the stream.

Taking a deep breath, we struggled up the steep embankment to the trail high above. Once there, I murmured, "That bear looks like it's been dead for a long time. And guess where that water goes. Right over the falls and into our water pipe."

Monty grimaced, "And we've been drinking it for weeks now."

Dad often boasted that we had the cleanest, coolest water in the entire park. That myth had just ended dramatically. We both wondered aloud how we could ever drink the creek water again. Quickly marking the spot on the trail, we turned and ran full speed to the cabin.

Monty spied Mom hanging clothes near the woodshed and shouted out, "Mom. You'll never guess what we found." The story spilled forth as we related our revolting discovery.

"Oh my," she responded. "Wait until your father hears about this." She paused. "And to think how he's always bragged about our water."

A couple of hours later, Dad hummed a cheerful tune as he arrived at the cabin following his day's work at Sun Point information station. In short order, he was informed of the rotting bruin in our water supply. Horrified and in a state of disbelief, he shed his uniform while he questioned us. How did we come across the dead bear? Was it far from the cabin?

It didn't take long for the three of us to reach the site of the bear's demise. Dad stood there staring at the bloated bruin. If possible, the stench seemed even worse than before. With a look of resolve, he stated, "That animal has to be removed. Now!" Then in disgust, he added, "I can't believe we've been drinking this water all summer."

Early the following day, Dad traveled to Saint Mary headquarters to explain the dilemma to District Ranger Don Barnum. Grinning from ear to ear, Don saw both the humor and the potential health hazard in our predicament.

In a matter of hours, we watched as four trail crewmen performed the unenviable tasks of retrieving the animal carcass. Wearing hip boots, they tied ropes around the hapless bear's remains, finally pulling it free of the log jam. Once at the creek's edge, they dragged the putrefied animal up the steep bank to the trail.

As fate would have it, two middle-aged women, clad in hiking shorts and boots, appeared at the same time. The first let out a horrified shriek. "Oh, my God! Its' a body." The two quickly reversed direction and double-timed it back up the trail.

Ever the gentleman, Dad took chase after them. A short time later he located the distraught hikers, sitting in their car in the parking lot.

Shaken, one woman spouted, "I've never seen a dead person before. That was awful."

Finally catching their attention, Dad carefully explained the situation. "Yes, ladies it was a body you saw, but it was not human. It was a bear that died in the creek some time ago."

With notable New England accents, the women thanked him for calming their fears. About the same time, the bear's remains, wrapped in canvas, were placed in the bed of a pickup truck waiting nearby. As the hikers watched the proceedings, Dad encouraged them to return to the trail and continue their hike to Baring Falls.

Our beloved Sun Camp Ranger Station was eventually torn down and its crumbling remains removed. Only the tall cottonwoods near the shoreline bear testimony to its former location. Likewise, the old Sun Point boat dock, in serious disrepair, was removed from its original site. Victims of time and weather, these structures are mentioned as monuments to a time and place now forgotten by most in Glacier Park's remarkable history.

One quickly responded, "No thanks. We've seen more than enough for one day." Their car's tires chirped as they sped out of the parking lot and disappeared down the Going-to-the-Sun Road.

Later, Dad confided that he had a difficult time imagining how anyone could possibly confuse a human corpse with that of a dead bear.

For several days to follow, we gathered water from the tap in one-gallon buckets. For good measure, a few drops of iodine were added as a disinfectant. Within a week's time, we felt comfortable using our water supply once more.

As a final note, we never heard Dad brag about our great drinking water again.

9

A CLOSE CALL ON SUN POINT

July 1953 - Mark and Monty Parratt — Sun Point

Suddenly a muffled scream broke the air. In the next moment, I watched Monty slide over the edge of a small cliff and disappear. In a frenzy of disbelief, I searched through the clouds of rising dust for a glimpse of him.

The spectacular red argillite cliffs of Sun Point presented a stunning contrast to the deep blue waters of Saint Mary Lake that early summer morning in 1953. My brother, Monty, and I set out to explore the area, always eager to expand our fishing possibilities. From the top of the promontory, the rusty rock slabs dropped abruptly into the icy waters of the lake, some 100 feet below. We were searching for a route that would take us down the steep walls to a tiny patch of rocky beach. If we could reach it, this hidden cove showed all the signs of becoming a prime fishing spot. Peering down from high atop Sun Point, we'd watched good sized lake trout lazily swimming near the surface of the pristine waters which lapped the shore.

Our backpacks, laden with fishing gear, and our hearts infused with boyhood enthusiasm, we approached the area that morning and began the slow descent toward our goal. Scattered limber pines became our handholds as we carefully worked our way down the cliffs. Within minutes, we'd reached the rock slabs that tilted almost vertically into the lake far below. A fleeting thought crossed my mind, "Mom would ground us for the rest of the summer if she knew what we were doing right now." A short vertical pitch lay ahead. From all appearances, if we could make our way across this obstacle, the nearby staircase cliffs would take us down to the beach.

As we inched across the rock face, the footing became increasingly more difficult. In no time, youthful eagerness gave way to pangs of fear. Quite suddenly, we both sensed we were in over our heads. We realized there was no way we could safely descend to the beach. Catching our breath, we made the decision to retrace our steps, hoping to return to secure ground.

It was then that I heard Monty cry, "No. Mark...I'm slipping." Helpless, I watched as he frantically grabbed for handholds on the steep pitch. Then, in eerie silence, he slid off the rock face, enveloped in a large cloud of dust. I could see nothing. There was no sign of my brother. In a quavering voice, I cried out, "Monty? Monty?" No sound. No response. My chest heaved with a fear I'd never felt before. Repeated calls seemed to vanish in the gusts of wind that tore at my clothing.

As the dust finally cleared, a hail of small rocks splashed into the lake. Peering downward, I spotted his small figure some ten feet below me. With a silent desperation, he grasped a small rock outcrop. His boots slipped beneath him with each of his furtive attempts to regain secure footing on the steep face. Breathless and paralyzed with fear, he could not speak.

In tears now, I shouted, "Monty, are you hurt?"

He shook his head in response. Clinging tenaciously to the handhold, his legs now swung in thin air. My mind raced as I tried to calm myself. Frightened, so frightened, he called in a hoarse whisper, "Mark, you've gotta help me."

How was I to reach him? I knew, in that moment, my young brother's life hung in the balance. I realized that I was the only one who could help him. My eyes darted back and forth across the rock face. At last, I spied an exposed root knotted there in the red shale. It anchored an aged pine off to my right and some six feet above where Monty hung. Apparently substantial, the tree formed a loop where it had grown into the rock. I called back to him, "Hang on. I'm coming to get you." I found a secure foothold and quickly made my decision. I would have to leap across a six foot chasm to reach the root. If I misjudged, my body would surely bounce off the cliffs before plummeting into the deep water below. This would spell Monty's demise as surely as my own. But for Monty's sake, I had to try.

I crouched low, took a deep breath and jumped, propelling

The cliffs around Sun Point.

myself across the deep void. As my body slammed against the root, I managed to grab it with both hands. Heart pounding, I glanced downward to find my brother suspended just a few feet below me.

Releasing my grasp with one hand and locking the other arm firmly around the root, I reached out to him, shouting, "Grab on, Monty!" With arms outstretched, we struggled to close the gap. Our fingers touched briefly and then slowly parted. I shall never forget the look of terror on his face. Never before in my young life had I felt so helpless. At once frightened and sick to my stomach, my muscles quivered. I was aghast at the thought of losing the best friend I had ever known.

My mind raced. At last, I decided to lock my ankles around the root. Rolling over on my stomach, my body now lay face down on the steeply pitched rock face. I clung there, inching my way toward Monty. Finally, I extended an outstretched hand in his direction. He slowly swung his body toward me, and then reached upward. Fingers touched and then, in one final determined effort, our hands clasped. My young brother now hung from the precipitous edge supported only by my arm. Summoning all the effort he could muster, the sturdy little fellow was able, hand over hand, to climb up my body. He scaled my frame, much as one would a ladder, until he reached our safe anchor. Grabbing onto his jeans, I then quickly curled my own body upward. We both lay there against the canted rock face, holding tightly to our mooring. Our gasps mingled with the mountain winds.

Breathless and visibly shaken, several moments passed before we found words. We'd managed our first step back to safety, but the leap across the six foot chasm still remained. With that behind us, we would finally be out of harm's way.

Faced with the daunting task, I realized I was simply too fatigued at this point to be certain of reaching the other side. In muffled tones, we discussed our only option; Monty would have to be the first to try. Although younger and considerably shorter, his athleticism was amazing. I felt certain he could do it.

He pulled himself up into a crouching position, hands and feet securely supported by the root beneath him. Then, without a word, he leapt across the span, snaring a pair of handholds on the opposite side. A small ledge below him conveniently provided footing. Safe at last, my young brother turned to me and smiled. Pride and relief flooded my senses.

With newfound confidence, Monty secured his grip on the ledge and called out, "Mark. Now, you can jump and grab onto me." I realized he was right. My flagging strength might not allow me to reach the rocky handholds. But, I could fling myself toward him, grasping my brother's clothing as I jumped. My only fear was that the blunt force of our collision would dislodge him. Trembling now, I pulled myself up into a crouch. Taking a last deep breath, I jumped.

In an instant, I was suspended in space. Nothing but rushing air surrounded me. Next, I felt my body slam into the small, solid form of my brother. With arms wrapped tightly around both of his legs, I slowly pulled myself upwards until I could plant my feet and reach handholds. We scrambled over the cliff's edge, together, and moved quickly to the familiar rock-strewn meadow beyond.

As we walked along the ridgeline, relief and disbelief alternately swept over us in waves. We hugged, and then finally allowed an outpouring of the powerful emotions we had held at bay during our flirtation with death. The dust that covered our faces quickly turned to muddy rivulets as tears flowed freely. Several moments passed. Then, without speaking and with our hands locked in a brotherly bond, we moved as one, retracing our steps back to the trail.

Hiking only a short distance, we stopped and sat down alongside the path, allowing our pent up thoughts to tumble forth. We talked about the poor decisions we'd made that day by venturing into unknown and unsafe terrain. In our haste to leave the cabin that morning, we'd also forgotten to bring rope, a major error when climbing. Our fate had nearly been decided on the cliffs of Sun Point. We promised one another never to take such risks again. In addition, we decided not to tell our mom about the troubling experience. Neither of us ever has.

We lost a share of our boyish innocence that day. Along with it went a certain sense of invincibility so typical in youth. Both our lives could well have ended in the icy depths of Saint Mary Lake that summer morning.

The lessons we'd learned would serve us well in the years to come. Whether hiking, climbing, or taking part in park service search and rescue operations through the summers that followed, we were never to forget our brush with death that windy day on Sun Point.

Sun Point was the former location of the Going-to-the-Sun Chalets, a popular tourist attraction during the 1920's and 1930's. A rustic boat dock served as an important stop for the passenger excursion launch that plied the waters of Saint Mary Lake. The weather-ravaged chalet was taken down in 1948, deemed unsafe after lying idle during the war years.

Pictured here is the Red Eagle parked at a reconstructed dock in the cove below Sun Point.

10
CAUGHT IN THE STORM

September 1953 - Mark and Monty Parratt – Saint Mary Lake

Powerful winds whipped Saint Mary Lake's cobalt blue waters forming whitecaps on the crests of large waves that pounded the shore. The caveat for anyone intent upon launching a small boat there is to respect the storms that roll down the valley, often with little or no warning. Over the years, the large mountain lake has been notorious for sudden disturbances which have capsized boats, sending sportsmen to watery graves. It must be said that the odds of surviving a plunge into such frigid waters are never good.

As a family, we had little experience boating on the lake. That was about to change soon in a life and death struggle against the awesome power of the driving winds and huge waves of Saint Mary Lake.

Sun Camp Ranger Station, our family's home for the summer, was located on the northern shore of upper Saint Mary Lake. Baring Creek tumbled into the lake only fifty feet from our bedroom window. Our sole access to the cabin was gained through one of two trails that dropped to the lake's edge from the Going-to-the-Sun Road. The only other alternative was to boat in from nearby Sun Point. The family soon discovered carrying our belongings and groceries to the cabin in packs was back-breaking and time-consuming work. It often took two or three days and dozens of trips just to bear a carload of groceries in to our mountain home.

Near the end of the previous summer, Dad declared, "You just wait, I'm going to figure out an easier way to do this next year." This was our father's fifth summer working as a seasonal ranger naturalist for the National Park Service. Our family loved the solitude provided by the isolated cabin, but we also wished fervently for easier access with the heavy loads. The following winter, Dad began his search for a solution to our problem and, eventually, he came up with an idea. "I think some sort of canoe would be a great help," he told us.

Consequently, the next summer found us with a shiny, new aluminum canoe strapped to the top of our Plymouth station wagon as we headed north. The sixteen-foot flat bottom craft was perfect for carrying a three-week supply of groceries from Sun Point to our cabin in a single voyage. Once we were settled in our snug home in the woods, Mom set out for Kalispell to buy groceries to satisfy the hearty appetites of her young family. The 150-mile jaunt consumed an entire day. Each shopping trip could be expected to fill two shopping carts to the brim, the stockpile required to supply our clan of five for several weeks. Since our cabin had no refrigeration, the bulk of the grocery list involved canned food and dry goods.

At the end of each day's shopping we prayed that the lake would be calm enough to portage the groceries by water. Driving winds, which roar down the lake for several days running, are an ever-present reality on the east side of Glacier's Continental Divide. Under siege from the constant gales, we were often forced to wait out a storm until calmer waters allowed us to bear our supplies to the cabin. When the winds did abate at the end of a shopping day, the entire family would spend an hour or more toting groceries from the family wagon down a steep trail of over one-hundred yards to the boat dock. After we loaded the canoe, the narrow craft typically rode very low in the water under the weight of the considerable supplies. By canoe, it would take us a good hour to reach the cabin's beachhead, oftentimes braving a moderate wind. The intrinsic reward for bringing home the groceries in a single canoe trip was a wonderful late dinner of fresh meat and vegetables. Fortunately, perishable foods like fruit and eggs lasted for days in our cold cellar beneath the kitchen floor.

That summer of 1953, we found the season rushing toward an end far too quickly. Cool evening temperatures and shorter days signaled the beginning of fall. Sprinklings of yellow leaves became more apparent on the tall cottonwood trees at the front of the cabin. The bugle of the bull elk signaled that it was time to pack up and leave our mountain paradise. Dad's naturalist work in Glacier ended each summer with the arrival of Labor Day weekend. Once again, it was time to head south on the long trek to our home in California. The teaching year for Dad and Mom would soon begin and the Parratt boys would undertake yet another year's schooling.

The day before our departure, we'd made two trips with the fully loaded canoe, moving a good share of our family's belongings to the

The Parratt Family paddles across Saint Mary Lake on a relatively calm day.

car. Dad later remarked that, "Today was pretty rough and windy, but it was doable." One final canoe trip the next morning would send us on our way.

After a well-earned night's rest, we awoke to a blustery, windy day. Following a hasty breakfast, it was a race to load our craft and paddle to Sun Point before the waves became unmanageable. As we carried gear to the beach, I noted that Dad's face wore a definite expression of concern as he continually surveyed the turbulent water.

Bidding us safe passage, Mom and younger brother, Smitty, turned and began the one-mile hike to the car. The worry on her face mirrored Dad's as she gave us a final wave and disappeared around a bend in the trail.

Tossing the last suitcase and duffel bag into the canoe, we secured the load, covering it with worn canvas tarps. As we climbed into the canoe, my younger brother, Monty, assumed the middle position, paddle in hand. I sat at the front of the canoe, grasping a second paddle. Dad slowly pushed off, then jumped into the seat at the rear. Above the roaring winds, he shouted, "This is it, boys. Paddle hard." The swells surged five feet in the air as the wind blew an icy mist into our faces. Strong gales quickly jettisoned our tiny craft far out from the shoreline. Within mere seconds, large waves tossed us recklessly about. Over the wail of the wind, Dad called out, "Left paddle! Left paddle!" Frantically, we attempted to do his bidding and the canoe slowly turned, heading directly toward the rocky Sun Point outcrop. Struggling, at last, we put the wind at our backs. Even so, it became increasingly difficult to keep the canoe on a straight course in the huge swells. The powerful gusts seemed to become more intense with each passing moment. Our canoe danced about, sliding sideways into the troughs of waves that grew deeper as we watched. It was plain to see we had a fight on our hands. Pangs of fear told us we were going to be a poor match for the fury that nature was about to unleash upon us.

Paddling frantically in the churning waters, a harsh reality suddenly struck us. We had lost control. With each successive wave, our craft took on more water. Tossed about in our tiny boat, each of us felt the frightening possibility that our canoe might soon swamp and capsize. The security provided by my tightly laced life vest did little to buoy my confidence. I knew, once in the lake, the incredibly cold water could snuff out a human life in a few short minutes. It suddenly became quite clear that there was no way the forces of nature were going to allow us to continue our present course to Sun Point.

In the next instant, a huge wave crested over us, all but swamping our wildly bobbing canoe. A sharp pang of fear resonated through my body. Above the howling wind, I could barely hear Dad shouting, "Pull harder! Harder!" In a final desperate attempt, Dad managed to turn the canoe toward the nearest shoreline, now some 400 feet distant. Filling with water, the over-burdened craft lumbered forward as wave after wave swept over us. There could be no mistake, we were slowly sinking. Monty and I struggled frantically, paddling toward the boulder-strewn shoreline.

The huge waves were thundering into the rocks as we drew closer to the water's edge. Suddenly, the bow bounced off a sunken outcrop and the canoe flipped over sideways, spilling us and our gear into the brutal backwash. As we bobbed about in the icy waters, cold pierced our clothing, quickly chilling our bodies with a numbing intensity. In the confusion, I was briefly aware of the sounds of crashing waves and the metallic thud of the canoe as it slammed against the large, jagged rocks along the shore.

In the midst of the confusion, a strong hand reached out and clutched my life vest. For a moment, my sluggish mind sprang back to keen awareness. Dad, a lifeguard in his college days, dragged me through the water toward the low, overhanging branch of a nearby pine. He had rescued Monty before me and I became aware of my younger brother desperately clinging to the swaying limb. The three of us tightly grasped the tree's foliage as our feet slipped repeatedly off the algae-covered rocks beneath. Finally, using the branch much like a lifeline, we managed to pull ourselves along it, our frantic efforts at last bringing us to rest on the beach. Breathless and exhausted, we lay there gasping alongside one another. Strangely, at the edge of my consciousness, the pounding of the waves brought to mind the sound of the Pacific Ocean surf, crashing against our native southern California coastline. In time, we managed to struggle to our feet. Then coming together, we embraced one another on that cold, windy beach. In that singular moment, I believe each of us sensed that a higher power had truly given us all a second chance at life that chilly day in early September.

After a few moment's rest, we helped Dad pull the battered canoe onto the beach, beyond the reach of the waves. Shivering from the intense cold, we trudged along the shoreline in search of our belongings, at last discovering one lone duffel bag. Apparently, the huge waves had drawn our water-soaked gear into the depths; even the canvas tarps had vanished. Dad pulled a soggy wool army surplus blanket from the battered bag. Wet or not, we huddled together under it, lying motionless on the shore for several minutes. Shared body heat slowly restored color to our pale, frightened faces. I glanced over at Dad and realized that tears streaked his face as he held us close. In a broken, trembling voice, he kept repeating, "We're O.K. now, boys. We're O.K." Seeing our father overcome by such emotion, Monty and I were soon in tears as well. Humbled by nature's fury, my young brother and I felt as though we had become men, too, if only for that one brief moment in time.

We knew that Mom was sure to be frantic by now. We were long since overdue at the Sun Point boat dock. Later, to our amazement, we discovered she had witnessed the entire drama from a vista high above us. With no one nearby to lend assistance, our hardy mother grabbed a rucksack from the car and stuffed it full of clothing and food. With our younger brother, Smitty, in tow, she scurried down the trail in our direction.

We suspected that the trail to Sun Point lay several hundred feet directly above where we had beached our craft. With no desire to return to the lake, our next challenge was to pull our canoe up the steep, forested slope to the narrow track. Dad fashioned three harness loops from a long rope that had been attached to the bow of our craft. With each of us straining at a loop, we slowly inched our way upward, dragging the canoe on its keel behind us. Using tree branches as handholds, we'd pull for a few moments, then, gasping for breath, we'd rest before the next effort. Two small cliffs proved a particular challenge, quickly sapping any of our flagging energy that remained.

In a short time, we were exhausted. About half way up the hillside, we recognized the sound of Mom's shouts coming from the trail high above. What a joy to hear that familiar voice once again. With renewed energy, we followed the calls and, at last, emerged from the dense forest to join her on the trail. Bruised, battered and covered with mud and pine needles, we finally struggled to stand upright. We followed Mom's gaze as it came to rest on the single, drenched duffel sitting forlornly in the battered canoe.

There on the trail, a tearful embrace bound us as one. All that mattered in that moment was that we were safe, together as a family once again. The missing gear would be replaced in time. Meanwhile, Mom pulled jackets and wool caps from the rucksack. The joy we felt at seeing the dry clothing helped warm bodies and hearts alike. As a bonus, she also pulled out a bag of sandwiches and a canteen of water which she'd packed earlier for a roadside meal. How we tore into that lunch. And, as she watched, strength and energy slowly ebbed back into her weather-worn family.

Finishing the meal, we gazed down upon the angry lake which had nearly taken our lives. Dad shook his head and sighed, "That is one tough, mean body of water. We are all so lucky to be out of there in one piece." Then, he began recounting the highlights of our errant voyage for Mom and Smitty.

By the time he finished, Mom's face wore a look of anguish. She pleaded, "Lloyd, please promise me that you won't try anything like this again."

His gaze dropped and he nodded, saying, "Now I realize we should've carried the canoe and the gear up the trail in the first place. Would have saved everyone a lot of worry and we'd have been on the road hours ago." He paused, then to reassure her, he stated,

"No, we'll be a lot more careful from now on, Grace, I give you my promise."

We carried the canoe in short shifts the remaining half mile to the car. At last, with the craft tightly strapped to the roof rack, we were ready to bid goodbye to our Glacier home and head south once again. I made a mental note of how good it felt to finally sit in the comfort of the car, safe from the assault of those brutal winds. A profound peace seemed to descend over us all as Dad turned our wagon out of the parking lot, heading toward Logan Pass, then, to points south.

11
THE SAINT MARY LAKE MONSTER

July 1954 – Saint Mary Lake Narrows

A venerable Canadian fisherman told us many stories of catching huge lake trout or mackinaw in the frigid waters of Saint Mary Lake. Old Man Dahl fished these haunts scores of times from the 1930's to the 1950's. Using a large wooden boat to troll the 200 foot depths, the ruddy-faced Norwegian became quite skilled at catching twenty-five pound trout. Never verified, however, were his colorful and imaginative tales of landing monster trout weighing fifty pounds or more. On occasion, Dahl docked his boat at our summer residence, the old Sun Camp Ranger Station. Mother always obliged by serving

Lloyd, Grace and Monty
in Old Man Dahl's wooden trolling boat.

him cookies and coffee.

My brother, Monty, and I were entranced by the craggy fisherman's stories. No matter how tall the tales, we accepted them as gospel and always begged for more.

Needless to say, the fantasies of two young brothers were greatly fueled by his accounts. One morning in early August, to our delight, Dahl took us fishing in his boat. It was a remarkable day on the lake. He shared his special fishing rigs and showed us many of his favorite trolling spots. At day's end, we gleefully raced into the cabin to display our catch, a pair of fifteen pound lake trout. Pumped up with excitement, we lay in our bunks and talked late into the night.

Old Man Dahl didn't return to the lake the following summer. Sadly, one night in the midst of the long, bleak Alberta winter, the old fisherman passed away in his sleep. Monty and I felt a dull void in our lives without him. We vowed, then and there, to fish the lake until one of us caught the big one. The catch would be dedicated to the fishing legend and our mentor, Old Man Dahl.

In early June of 1954, the Glacier Park Boat Company launched the new passenger cruiser, the *Red Eagle*, on Saint Mary Lake. Located at Rising Sun, the company added several fifteen foot wooden boats as well. The small craft could be rented as either rowboats or fitted with small outboard engines. I was hired that summer to sell tickets for the daily cruises and to handle the small boat rentals.

Thankfully, the boat dock at Rising Sun is partially protected from the lake's legendary high winds. Even so, with good reason, there were many days during the summer when gale force conditions compelled us to suspend our rental operations altogether. The lake had a long and storied history of capsizing small craft, sending fishermen to watery graves.

In sharp contrast, there were the rare instances when the lake remained calm and mirror-like for the entire day. One such occasion occurred July 18, 1954 and was destined to hold the most exciting fishing adventure of my young life. Business was slow, so owner, Art Burch, gave me the use of a rental outboard during my lunch hour.

Mark Parratt at the Rising Sun boat ramp.

I was eager to try some new heavy duty fishing gear, a gift from my parents on the occasion of my thirteenth birthday.

The small Johnson outboard purred along as I maneuvered the boat into an area of the lake known as *the narrows*. This geographic feature is the result of a large limestone outcrop that juts into the waters near Rising Sun. A corresponding ridge on the opposite shore reaches out to create the narrowing.

Once in position, I cut the motor and hastily rigged my deep sea rod and reel. The shiny new reel was spooled with 600 feet of well-used fifty pound test leaded line. A steel wire leader was attached to a large red and white Daredevle lure. I snapped a two pound leaded weight onto an extension line and fired up the motor. As the boat entered the narrows, I released the drag on the reel and tossed the rigging overboard. I watched the lure tumble down through the clear water for some fifty feet, then disappear into the darkness.

A short time later, I felt a bounce as the leaded weight struck bottom. Rapidly reeling in about five feet of line, I kept the weight from snagging the lake floor and then set the drag on the reel. With fifty foot increment marks on the line, I guessed the trolling depth at 200 feet. Old Man Dahl favored the narrows as a prime fishing spot, realizing the large lake trout spent the majority of the summer months in these deeper, cooler waters. As the motor slowly droned on, my thoughts drifted to the crafty old fisherman, and I felt sure he was out there somewhere smiling down upon me.

With one hand steering the boat, I held the fishing rod in the other, locking it between my knees. The warm air hovering on the lake, combined with the odor of the smoky two-stroke engine, lulled my senses into a dream-like state. What a beautiful day to be out on the water.

Suddenly, my pole sprung downward, the tip slamming against the side of the boat. I tightened my grasp and jerked upward on the rod, a flush of excitement coursing through my body. Was it a strike? I felt only the normal drag resistance of the leaded line and the rigging. The euphoria of the moment faded as I reeled in a few more feet of line and whipped the pole upward a few times. No response. I guessed that the rigging had temporarily snagged on a rock.

Once more, I released enough line to feel the bounce of the weight on the lake floor. Again, I tightened the tension on the line. I realized it would soon be time to call it quits and head back to work at the dock. It would take time to reel in the 500 feet of trolling line which now angled into the depths behind the boat.

As I reached toward the knob on my reel, my pole suddenly bent double, slamming hard against the railing. Instinctively, I pulled sharply upward to set the hook. Immediately, a powerful throbbing shook the pole. I felt certain I'd hooked a big mackinaw. Youthful adrenaline surged through my body. As the fish struggled beneath me, the tip of the pole continued to splash the water's surface. Quickly cutting the motor, I swung the propeller out of the water. Using all my strength, I was barely able to keep the pole high enough to clear the edge of the craft.

Slowly, a series of clicking sounds told me the big fish had begun to pull line from my reel. I continued to tighten the drag as the sounds slowed, and then stopped. Guessing there were fewer than twenty-five feet of line remaining on the reel, I tightened the drag to a full stop. The aged line would simply have to hold. I could only hang on and hope. The pole bent double as the powerful creature continued to struggle. I winced with every tug, expecting the line to snap at any moment.

The day grew warmer as the summer sun bore down upon the still waters. As I caught a quick glance at the nearby shoreline, I realized the boat was moving. The mackinaw was towing my craft slowly up the lake. Grabbing my canteen with one hand, I gulped down the last of my water. Perspiration poured off my face as the intense afternoon sun beat down upon me. It was hot. Really hot.

Suddenly, the fish changed direction and began to pull the line under the boat. I feared the splintered wood on the weathered keel would surely abrade the line, eventually causing it to snap. Quickly, I backed off the drag on the reel. Guiding the pole carefully around the bow of the boat, I gained a better position for the contest. Now, the great fish began towing the boat slowly down the lake in the opposite direction. Taut line moved through the glassy surface parting small clusters of floating pine pollen.

With a glance at my watch, I guessed that I'd been hooked up with the fish for a good forty-five minutes. Would the monster ever tire? I was dehydrated and exhausted. The muscles in my back convulsed and my arms became limp with the tension.

A sense of urgency began to overtake me. I desperately wanted to pull this fish off the bottom and bring it in. With repeated attempts, I reeled in ten to fifteen feet of line, only to quickly lose it again to the powerful thrashing of the trout.

My mind wandered. Then, abruptly, my thoughts returned to the boat dock. Reality struck. I was scheduled to sell tickets for the afternoon boat cruise. I was already late. Beyond the narrows, I spied a faint line of passengers boarding the *Red Eagle*. I promptly decided I was not going to lose this fish. This was a battle I simply had to finish. I could feel my face burning from the intense sunlight reflecting off the still water. Shortly, I heard the rumble of its engines as the *Red Eagle* approached.

A familiar voice called out to me from the flying bridge of the cruiser. Louie Cousineau, the boat's captain hailed me. With the launch idling some 200 feet off my stern, he shouted, "The boss says that you'd better bring this one in. You're on company time now and this will be darned nice for our business." Glacier Park Boat Company's owner, Art Burch, had been following my progress with binoculars for several minutes from his vantage point on the dock. His suspicions told him that I'd tied onto a good-sized fish. Passengers on the tour cruise lined up along the railings to cheer me on. The *Red Eagle* slowly moved away and, at last, became a tiny speck in the distance. The encouragement was the very tonic I needed.

With renewed resolve, I pulled the pole upward and rapidly reeled in a few feet of line. By continually repeating the process, I managed to turn the fish toward the boat, coaxing it from the lake bottom. The once powerful tugs were less frequent now. I sensed the great fish was beginning to tire. With smooth cranks on the reel, the line markers moved slowly upward from the depths. Giving a strong kick, the powerful fish once again passed under the boat. No longer a stranger to its tactics, I stuck the pole in the water and guided the taut line following it. I continued to counter as the fish made three more such runs. I was now progressing at a steady pace. It seemed as if the trout and I were matching wits in a game of survival. There had to be less than fifty feet of line in the water. I could feel my heart pulsing strongly in my chest.

Harboring visions of being jerked out of the boat by a mighty mackinaw, I braced my legs against the hull. Peering over the edge, my eyes followed the shards of sunlight as they danced in the blue depths. Suddenly, several brilliant flashes pierced the water as the gigantic fish spun wildly to the surface. Water depth tends to magnify the size of a fish...and, to my boyish eyes, this monster appeared to be as long as the boat. My excitement grew with each passing moment. Slowly bringing the big fish alongside, I began to tremble uncontrollably. I was absolutely stunned by the immensity of this lake trout. He was mine and, amazingly, I was the victor in what is generally the toughest part of the battle.

With one hand cradling the pole, I slowly slid the gaff hook into the water. As the large hook moved near its massive head, the mackinaw thrashed its tail and made a final run, which took it several feet from the boat. Once more, I slowly brought the great fish alongside. Slipping the gaff hook into the water, I aimed at the trout's large gill slit. I connected. Spending my last shred of strength, I dragged the monster into the boat. Jumping atop the struggling fish, I waited for the thrashing to subside.

Too exhausted to rise, I gazed at the sky as I lay beside the quivering behemoth. Occasionally, I'd turn my head to examine the prize…as well as to make certain I wasn't dreaming. The battle with the big fellow had taken just over two hours. All consuming was the ultimate thrill of landing one of the big ones. Keen memories of Old Man Dahl overtook me. I knew he was proud. Truly, this was his kind of fish.

With arms still weak and trembling, I lowered the propeller housing into the water. I pulled on the engine recoil rope several times. The little motor finally sputtered to life, and I turned the boat toward the distant shoreline. The glow I felt far surpassed the bright sunshine spilling around me.

As I neared the dock, Art Burch stepped forward to congratulate me. A short time later, he hefted the huge fish out of the boat, laying it gently in the back of his pickup. I eagerly climbed in beside him and we drove the half mile to the Rising Sun General Store, site of the only reliable scale in the area.

The massive lake trout weighed in at *42 pounds, 8 ounces and measured 49 inches* in length. With an immense head, its greatest girth totaled a whopping twenty-seven inches. Later, we were to learn that the lake trout was the largest fish ever caught in Glacier National Park. That record remains to this day.

Word of the big fish spread through the Saint Mary Valley like Montana mosquitoes. It wasn't long before the news reached my father, ranger naturalist Lloyd Parratt, who arrived with camera in hand a short time later. Filled with pride, Dad took several pictures to preserve the moment for posterity. As the fish lay on large blocks of ice near the meat locker, curious onlookers and fishermen filed past with looks of admiration. Absorbing the accolades, I sat in a nearby chair and gazed at my catch. One local fisherman tapped me on the shoulder and said, "You are one lucky guy." Motioning toward the massive trout, he said, "I've been fishing this lake since the early 1950's and I've never seen anything even half this size. Congratulations, young man."

I thought, "Well, luck was certainly part of it...but, the know-how gained at the knee of Old Man Dahl was what really enabled it to happen." Even as a youngster, I sensed that this would be the fishing achievement of my lifetime.

We dressed out the fish and carefully examined the contents of its stomach. Here, we discovered five fish in various states of digestion. The largest, a two-pound cutthroat trout, illustrated the predatory nature of the lake trout. The other fish included three good-sized mountain whitefish and a smaller rainbow trout.

As luck would have it, the next evening was the date of the annual eastside potluck dinner. All the Saint Mary park service employees were invited. My monster trout was filleted and cooked up in a large outdoor barbecue pit. The rich, reddish orange meat had a flavor similar to choice wild salmon. The entire fish vanished as over fifty diners devoured the tender flakes. There could be no doubt. The tasty fillets were a resounding hit.

The big fish later gained honorable mention in the 1954 *Field and Stream* magazine's trophy list for lake trout. The big one remains among the larger lake trout ever caught in the State of Montana, possibly a state record, but never submitted. The current record-holding lake trout caught in Flathead Lake is *42.69 pounds and 42.5 inches* and is virtually identical in girth and weight. At *49 inches long,* we'll consider the Saint Mary Lake monster as the unofficial record

Monty Parratt stands proud next to his brother Mark with the Saint Mary Lake Monster.

for the longest trout ever caught in Montana.

During the many summers that followed, Monty and I continued to fish Saint Mary Lake. Occasional mackinaws in the fifteen to twenty pound range were our largest catches.

We feel certain they are down there...the really big ones...lurking in those dark, cold depths. Why not give it a try? Perhaps Old Man Dahl will smile upon you one day for the catch of a lifetime.

12
A SLAP IN THE NIGHT

August 1956 – Sun Camp Ranger Station

During our seventeen summers in Glacier, we learned to respect the animals with whom we shared this mountain paradise. On a warm July evening, Dad was returning home from an illustrated evening program he'd presented at Saint Mary. The song of crickets serenaded endlessly as the scent of cottonwoods wafted along on a gentle breeze. Upon arriving at the trailhead, he donned his pack and began the traverse down the steep trail to the cabin with flashlight in hand. The glow from his beam bounced off the familiar features along the trail he knew so well. He passed the intersection

Ranger Lloyd Parratt.

to Baring Falls and then proceeded down the last hundred yards to our cozy log home nestled in the woods. The eerie sound of a loon on the lake pierced the quiet evening. He thought, "What a remarkable place this is."

In the distance, he could now see a dim light glowing in the cabin window. He smiled, thinking of the loved ones waiting for him there. Suddenly, without warning, the tranquility of the evening was shattered. He was stunned by a sharp blow to the back of his leg. Shifting his flashlight toward a rustling noise at the side of the trail, the beam briefly illuminated a large porcupine disappearing into the shrubbery. Stung by searing pain, he limped over to a nearby tree stump and quickly sat down. Directing the beam of light toward the back of his leg, he discovered a mass of porcupine quills piercing his trousers and deeply imbedded in his right calf. The suspect animal, hidden by trailside shrubbery, had given Dad a quick defensive slap on the leg with its armed tail and then retreated.

Slowly, Dad limped the remaining few yards to the cabin. His expression of anguish as he opened the door sent Mom rushing to his side. Bleeding and grimacing with pain, he slowly made his way to the bedroom with the help of his family. Monty and I stood by as Mom began to treat his injuries. Unable to raise dad's pant leg, she quickly found her scissors, cutting the quills in half to release their internal pressure. A total of twenty-five of the needle-sharp spears pierced his leg. Some, she guessed, were driven into his flesh a half-inch. Knowing that any movement could drive the quills even deeper, she kept him still.

Working under the flickering light of a Coleman lantern, she began the painful process of removing the quills, one at a time, using Dad's fishing pliers. The task took a good two hours. Mom liberally applied Mercurochrome in order to prevent infection. Her labors done, she wrapped the badly swollen leg in gauze.

There would be no sleep for Dad that night. His occasional moans could be heard from the next room where we three got little sleep ourselves.

At daybreak, Mom put the old crank phone into service and

called the Saint Mary headquarters to inform them of the situation. With a genuine risk of infection from the multiple puncture wounds, it was agreed that Dad should seek medical attention as soon as possible. The plan was to canoe out to Sun Point, which would result in the shortest walk on the painful limb.

As we consumed a quick breakfast, the sky became grey and a strong wind blew in, churning up the waves across the lake's surface. Within the span of half an hour, the weather had changed drastically from calm to tempest conditions.

We agreed it had become far too dangerous to use the canoe. Our only option was to do all we could to assist Dad on the agonizing walk up the steep, half-mile trek to the car. The usual brisk hike of fifteen minutes now became a tedious one-hour ordeal for our father.

With Mom at the wheel, we sped to the nearest doctor, stationed at the Many Glacier Hotel some forty miles away. There, the medic gave Dad a tetanus booster shot, a course of penicillin and the warning to go home and rest.

The puncture wounds healed without infection and Dad gladly returned to his naturalist duties. During the many summers that followed, our family acknowledged a heightened respect for the quilled beasts who roamed our beloved mountains.

13

THE WAR WAGON

June 1959 – Belly River Ranger Station

The sun fell softly on the shoulders of the great bear. Her long, sharp claws plunged into the recesses of the ground squirrel's den as her curious cubs watched nearby. A short distance from the grizzlies, a strange wagon track led through the aspen-fringed meadow.

The summer of 1959 had finally arrived. I was eighteen at last, brimming with confidence and eager for my first summer's work with the park service. Early June found me in fire school at West Glacier headquarters. Here, fireguards and rangers were trained in mapping, compass work, fire suppression, equipment use and a host of other skills. After several days of rigorous training, instructors deemed me qualified to begin work as a fireguard.

Assigned to the remote Belly River Ranger Station, my supervisor would be the controversial backcountry ranger, Joe Heimes. Heimes, I learned, had spent the past twenty-two years as a ranger at Belly River and considered it his turf. He greatly resented what he considered outside interference from park headquarters. The crusty veteran reportedly had the demeanor of a military drill instructor, demanding nothing short of perfection from his employees. To my dismay, I learned that some of his previous fireguards had quit after only a few weeks. Fireguards already assigned to other park locations and a few instructors were already taking bets as to how long I'd last.

Belly River's backcountry outpost can be found six miles south of the Canadian border. Located in the park's northeastern corner, its most direct access is by way of a trail that intermingles with a washboard wagon road. Both roughly follow the course of the northward-flowing Belly River. This rugged wilderness area is known to be spectacular and, at times, unforgiving.

Cool breezes wafted through the early morning as our pickup truck began the long trek over the Continental Divide, then northward to the Canadian border. By mid-morning, we arrived at a wide pullout within sight of the Chief Mountain Customs Station. The trailhead sign for Belly River was visible near the forest's edge. A wave of excitement swept through me as I pondered the adventures and uncertainties that lay ahead. This was the day I was destined to meet the legendary Joe Heimes.

With a few personal items loaded in my backpack, I thanked my driver and struck out for the trailhead. Beads of sweat gathered on my forehead as I made my way down the scores of switchbacks in the warm summer sun. In the distance, I caught sight of the Belly River wending its way through cottonwoods and quaking aspen. A short time later, the trail led me out of the dense forest and onto a broad meadow.

There, in a clearing near the river, stood a strange-looking wagon hitched to two good-sized draft horses. Oddly, the rig was equipped with the axles and tires of an automobile, yet it held the standard seating of a buckboard wagon. Painted dark green, it boasted a trim of bright red, causing it to look like an escapee from a gypsy camp.

Sitting next to the wagon was a four-wheel drive park service truck. Heavily loaded, it held my personal gear and a two-week supply of grub for the employees at the ranger station. Earlier that morning, Al Hoover, a ranger from Saint Mary, had driven the venerable supply truck to a point of rendezvous with the wagon.

I crossed the meadow and quickly made my way toward the group. Off to one side stood Joe Heimes. Without expression, he looked me over, the stub of a handmade cigarette held tightly between his lips. I guessed the grizzled park ranger to be somewhere in his fifties. Set in the midst of a ruddy face, his bulging eyes seemed to penetrate my very soul.

After a moment's hesitation, I summoned the courage to approach. Facing him, I smiled and said, "Hello, Mr. Heimes. I'm your new fireguard."

He responded gruffly, "And here, I thought you were just another tourist." Taking a puff on his cigarette, he slowly circled me. Next, he growled, "Oh no, they've gone and done it again. I've got me another damn, skinny, greenhorn rookie to break in." Then, after a few moment's silence, he squinted and grumbled, "Boy, are you sure you're eighteen?"

Trembling slightly, I stated, "Yessir. I am." Riddled with fear, I realized I was hyperventilating. My stomach churned as I willed myself to take a deep breath.

Heimes turned on his heel and strode toward the wagon. In his wake, Al Hoover took me to one side, clapping a fatherly arm around my shoulder. With a level gaze, he gently warned, "Don't get too bothered about old Joe. He's kind of temperamental this

The War Wagon rests at the Belly River Ranger Station.

time of year. Give it some time and he'll kind of grow on you."

A week of unusually warm weather had heightened the rate of snowmelt in the high country, changing the normally docile Belly River into a raging torrent. Paralleling the watercourse, a hiking trail and a wagon track led the five miles to the outpost.

Later, I would learn that a memo from park headquarters had decreed that wagon crossings at high water were hazardous, preferring instead the transport of goods by mule pack train. In spite of this, Heimes insisted the three river crossings that day would not be a problem for his team. As was often the case, Joe pled his cause and won. As we prepared to leave, Hoover again warned of the dangers of the swift current. Defensively, Heimes shot back, "Well, I got up here O.K., didn't I? Gotta get this wagon

Saint Mary Sub-District Ranger Robert Frauson during an inspection of the Belly River Ranger Station.

back to the ranger station somehow."

Without further comment, the supplies from the pickup were loaded into the wagon and tied down with canvas tarps. Since refrigeration wasn't available at Belly River, provisions consisted of either canned or boxed dry goods. As we bore the heavy boxes to the wagon, I guessed that the canned goods, alone, must weigh several hundred pounds.

Finally, the job was done and Joe commanded impatiently, "O.K., greenhorn, get in." As I climbed onto the seat beside him, he chimed, "You'd best hang on because this is gonna be a rough ride. Oh, and just so you know, I call this rig the *War Wagon*."

With a parting nod to Al Hoover, Heimes snapped the reins and called out to his lead horse, Rube. We were on our way. I looked back wistfully at the small figure waving to us in the distance.

Suddenly, I realized I had never felt quite so alone. A million thoughts swirled through my mind. The uncertainty of my situation was intimidating, to be sure. Somehow, I sensed this day would mark the beginning of a summer I would never forget.

My wandering thoughts quickly focused as the wagon approached the first river crossing. The horses willingly responded to Joe's commands and surged forward through the swift waters with surprising ease. I couldn't help but admire the way my boss handled the team. The large animals seemed to anticipate his every command. Then, for a brief moment, the wagon lost contact with the rocky river bottom. As it slid sideways, borne by the swift current, the horses muscled their way forward. After considerable effort, we reached the opposite bank.

Further along the trail, we forded the river a second time, without incident. However, during the final crossing, the wagon dropped abruptly into a deep sinkhole and began to float sideways with the downstream current. The horses struggled to regain their footing as I watched the water lap over the sides of the wagon bed. With a quick glance, I noted that Joe wore a look of concern as he continued to steady the reins and call out encouragement to the team. The situation was, at once, frightening and strangely exciting.

Then, with a sharp lurch, Rube stumbled on the rocky bottom, pulling the other horse off his feet. The torrent carried the wagon and team downstream for several yards. Muscles straining, the horses finally regained their footing near the opposite bank. I stifled a sigh of relief.

The War Wagon came to a sudden stop at a steep angle and we found ourselves surrounded by several large boulders at the river's edge. Our brief victory was dimmed by the sudden realization that a goodly portion of our food supplies had been tossed over the side of the wagon in the mêlée. We both watched to see one of our tarps and several boxes of cereal float away down the river. What remained of the colorful cans and boxes was strewn about the shoreline. After a pause, Joe muttered, "Damn. Now, we've really got ourselves in a fix."

Still a bit unsettled from the turbulent crossing, I glanced about quickly and realized what he meant. The wagon trail lay atop a sheer embankment some eight feet above us. As we sat there in the hot summer sun, our dilemma became all too obvious.

Joe mused, "You see those boulders over there? It's for sure the War Wagon ain't gonna make it over those. She'd prob'ly break an axle or worse. The way I figure it, the only way out of this mess is to move the rig along the edge of the water 'til we get to that level spot where the bank slopes up to the trail, easy like."

Wide eyed, I looked at him. "So, what do we do now?"

"Well, we gotta carry every damn can of food and all the rest up to the trail. Then, if we get the team and wagon up there, we gotta load everything up again." Heimes added, "One thing for sure. You're gonna earn your government pay today, boy."

Sweating profusely, it took us an hour to collect our supplies and carry them up to the spot Joe had indicated. With the job done, we sat there, exhausted, amongst the carnage of wet cardboard boxes and dented cans.

Joe mused, "I'll bet we lost a third of our food down the river. We're gonna come up a little short on grub the next few weeks."

To my relief, the two large duffel bags containing my clothes and personal items were still tied behind the seat and had remained in the wagon.

I stood on the bank and watched as Joe climbed aboard and began the daunting task of moving the rig from the riverbed to the trail above. With a quick snap of the reins, he yelled, "Hee yaw. Go, Rube!"

The wagon slowly crept over the rocks and promptly wedged itself between two formidable boulders. No matter how hard the horses strained, the balky wagon refused to budge. In resignation, Heimes dragged forth several short planks that he kept tied inside the wagon box. After strategically placing them between tires and boulders, Joe hopped aboard and, once more, urged the horses forward. With a sudden lurch, the wagon was free. Bouncing and sliding, it finally reached the trail above.

With wagon and supplies now side by side, we slowly began the reloading process. It was then that I noticed a fishy odor filling the air. Apparently, the rough crossing had caused a can of salmon to split open, spilling its contents over the damp supplies.

Next, I noted movement out of the corner of my eye and looked up to see a bear with two cubs in the distance. As they ambled toward us, the sow stopped, rose up on her hind legs and sniffed the breeze. The cubs huddled close behind her. No doubt, she'd picked up the tantalizing scent of our salmon.

About the same time, Joe spotted the bears and blurted, "Well, hell's bells. Now we got grizzlies to deal with. With that busted can of salmon, we're baited up like a bear trap. Grizzlies ain't nothin' but a nose on four legs, anyway. You'd better get in and hang on. We're gonna have to make a run for it."

Swiftly, we leapt aboard the wagon. Joe snapped the reins and the horses lunged forward. Soon, we were hurtling down the trail at full speed. I watched in disbelief as we careened toward the bears. We were actually charging the grizzlies.

As the wagon approached, the cubs ran off the side of the road into a patch of aspen. Refusing to be intimidated, the mother reared up and held her ground. Next, she dropped onto all fours, and then bounded straight toward us. For a split second, it appeared as though wagon and grizzly would surely collide. But then, at the last possible moment, the bear veered from the path.

At once, both horses reared up, front hooves pawing the air. In their wake, the wagon tilted onto two wheels. It hovered there for a moment, then came crashing down and slid sideways for several feet. With notable effort, Joe managed to gain control of the team. Miraculously, the provisions remained in place. Once again, we were under way.

Glancing back through a veil of dust, I saw the sow rear up one last time, then turn and mount a small hill. From her vantage point, she gave us a final look, then scurried out of sight with her cubs in tow.

Somewhat triumphantly, Joe remarked, "Well. We got that one behind us. I think we're in the clear. The ranger station isn't far now."

At this point, all I could do was nod my head. Later, Joe confided he'd spotted a number of different grizzlies in the meadow around the station during late spring. He'd also seen abundant bear tracks and scat on his backcountry patrols. In a passing remark, he'd noted, "This could be an interesting year for bears." As the summer wore on, his sage words became prophetic.

Approaching our destination, Joe's gruff exterior seemed to soften somewhat and, with a smile, he admitted, "Maybe I was a bit hard on you earlier, greenhorn. I'd guess all those summers spent growing up in the park could be helpful." Then, he volunteered, "Say, your paperwork mentioned that you worked for the Glacier Park Boat Company a few summers back. You wouldn't happen to know anything about motors, would you? We've got a balky generator up here that seems to have a mind of its own."

His satisfaction grew as I confessed that working on small engines was one skill with which I felt quite comfortable. Apparently, the generator's carburetor repair kit and new ignition parts had been sitting in his office for two years. The fact that I had the generator running smoothly by noon the following day earned me a guarded respect that lasted the rest of the summer.

At last, we drew to a halt behind the ranger station and set about the task of unloading. With the wagon empty, I was granted the rest of the day to settle in and explore the area around the station. As we parted, Joe snapped, "I'll see you at the office at 8:00 A.M. tomorrow," and then added, "Be on time!"

As the summer wore on, I found my new home at Belly River starkly beautiful. The ranger station sat on the edge of a large, open meadow at the base of Lee Ridge. A barbed wire fence, strung between wooden posts, marked the perimeter. Horses stood in a corral near an aged barn which had been the original ranger station. Lining a dense fringe of forest to the rear stood three small cabins. The first in the string was to be mine for the summer. The second housed the three-man trail crew.

I quickly fell to the task of cleaning my cabin, unloading duffels and arranging my gear. After surveying my meager food supply, I resolved to supplement my diet with fish. Monty and I had explored the Belly River country in previous summers, discovering some excellent fishing holes near the station.

As I swept my cabin, a pair of wood rats snarled at me from behind a small woodpile next to the cook stove. I escorted the interlopers out the door with my broom. A resident porcupine who lived beneath the cabin, had chewed a hole in the floor. One of my first tasks was to cover the opening, preventing access for the local rat and mouse population.

A single room, my quarters housed a bed, a kitchen table and chair, a rustic dresser and the cook stove. Two Coleman kerosene lanterns provided light for the evening hours. A classic 1923 General Electric telephone hung on the wall. It struck a nostalgic chord in its similarity to the one at our family cabin during my boyhood days at Saint Mary Lake.

As the day drew to a close, an orange glow bounced off Gable Mountain and the surrounding peaks.

The day's adventures had brought on a hearty appetite and my Spam sandwich, chips, and a dented can of peaches hit the spot. My final tasks for the day were a trek to the outhouse and to nearby Gable Creek for a supply of ice cold water. A rustling sound from the bushes caught me by surprise as I knelt to fill my bucket. Quickly swinging my flashlight about, I caught sight of the resident porcupine going about his nocturnal rounds.

Darkness fell as I lay on my bunk. I was overcome with a sense of wonder at the day's adventures, coupled with intense anticipation of what tomorrow would bring. My last memory was the haunting echo of a Great Horned Owl as I quickly slipped into a deep, dreamless sleep.

14

HOW'D YOU LOSE
YOUR HORSE?

My horse seemed to hover in mid-air and then lost his footing on the rocky slope. For a brief moment, panic gripped me as my body slammed brutally to the ground. I was alone, and for the moment, I couldn't move or breathe. My mind raced, "Is this it? Does my life end here on this lonely mountain?"

After my exciting arrival at Belly River Ranger Station via Joe Heimes' *War Wagon*, my work as a fireguard began in earnest. My diverse job description that summer included organizing and tending a small fire cache and patrolling backcountry trails. Additionally, I ran the fire weather station, worked with horses, repaired downed telephone lines and restrung the barbed wire fences which circled the perimeter of the ranger station.

Heimes was one of the few remaining old-time backcountry rangers. A crusty fellow with a predictably dour attitude, Joe was a loner in the true sense of the word. At the onset, he made it clear to me that his instructions would be given only once. Consequently, a greenhorn had to learn fast and rely on his instincts. I can honestly state that, from first instruction, I was strictly on my own. Fresh out of high school, I certainly didn't arrive at Belly River with many specialized backcountry skills. My saving grace was that every previous summer of my young life had been spent in Glacier with my family. My father, as a seasonal ranger naturalist, had taught me many of the basic skills necessary for day-to-day living in the backcountry. I was to thank him many times over the summer for the guidance he had given me.

In those days, most sections of the park used an antiquated 1920's General Electric telephone system which relied on short and long ring sequences to make calls within a given area. Everyone in the vicinity who had a phone would listen carefully for his particular ring. Needless to say, this arrangement represented the ultimate party line, where many a personal call could be overheard by anyone bent on eavesdropping. The Belly River phone system included connections to the ranger station, my fireguard cabin, and the customs station as well as the remote Bear Mountain Fire Lookout.

A thick wire strand, the primitive line stretched between a few short poles around the ranger station complex and then disappeared into the nearby forest where ceramic insulators attached it to living trees. Lines generally paralleled established trails and were suspended some twenty-five to thirty feet above the forest floor, anchored to a tree every hundred feet or so.

One of my first tasks upon arriving at Belly River that summer was to repair the weather-worn phone line that ran from the ranger station to Bear Mountain Fire Lookout. The project was divided into two sections. The first included a relatively flat, heavily timbered trail section that ran for four miles from the ranger station to the lookout trail intersection. The second segment, although short in overall distance, involved a very steep climb from the intersection up to the lookout tower. The tower, itself, was perched on a ridge a couple thousand feet below the 8,840 foot sentinel appropriately known as Bear Mountain.

The previous winter had been particularly harsh. Ferocious storms that lashed the area had felled numerous trees. The fallen trees, in turn, had snapped the telephone line in a number of places. After two weeks of hard work, I was very close to finishing the splices on the four mile stretch of line that led to the trail intersection. I reckoned that, in a single day's time, I could finish the task in a few hours and then begin work on the final stretch which zigzagged its way up to the lookout. With any luck, my work should be finished by day's end.

I finished my breakfast and saddled up Red, a trusty old steed who had spent many years plying the backcountry trails. Packing his saddlebags, I methodically stowed coiled sections of phone line, an assortment of repair equipment, my lunch, a water canteen, and last of all a rain slicker. I felt good about the day that lay ahead. By late afternoon, the phone line to the lookout would be in working order. Joe would be pleased.

It was a cool, crisp morning as I rode out of the corral and slowly headed up the trail. The pungent fragrance of cottonwoods and cow parsnip melded into a heavenly mountain perfume. Crossing the Belly River, we gradually made our way into the shade of the dense forest, plodding lazily along the sun-dappled trail. Shortly before the lookout trail intersection, I spied a large fallen spruce. The massive tree had completely downed about three hundred feet of line, snapping it in two places

I climbed off my horse and hitched pole climbers to each of my work boots. Clamped to the inside of each boot, the climber was a belted strap which housed a sharp spike approximately four inches long. By jamming the lineman's spikes into a tree, one could scale its trunk in moments to splice a broken line. In addition, a wide leather safety harness was drawn around the tree and then clipped to a belt which encircled my waist. The lineman's belt provided a valuable safeguard each time I climbed or descended a tree, vital protection in case the spikes slipped. The rig had kept me from falling at least twice over the past several days. I'd discovered that trees which were wet or small in diameter proved to be particularly hazardous. Another danger was the possibility of driving a spike into one's lower leg. This was a very painful error made by some park service workers through the years and was guaranteed to quickly end a day's labors.

I worked for three hours without pause, splicing the breaks. I found the work was tedious and exhausting, but brought with it a real sense of satisfaction. Completing the last repair, I heaved a sigh. I rested a moment, then decided it was time to tackle the final section which led to the lookout. This day had passed more quickly than I'd planned. Climbing aboard old Red, I noted the weather had begun to deteriorate as gusty winds tugged at my clothing. Ignoring the sudden change, I was determined to reach the lookout before the day was done. One last stretch faced me before I could head home. I glanced up, my eyes following a long series of switchbacks. The narrow track zigzagged over steep, rocky patches, finally ending at timberline. The lookout was in sight.

The thought of a well-earned supper and a good night's rest spurred me on. Soon I'd be headed back down the trail to my snug cabin. A sense of satisfaction began to settle over me, when suddenly, I was distracted by something in the trail ahead. I tugged at the reins, bringing Red to an abrupt halt. Several mounds of steaming bear scat sent chills up my spine. Droppings this fresh surely meant that a bear was only minutes ahead of me on the trail. My heart quickened. Cautiously, I urged Red forward. The old horse seemed skittish and purposefully made a wide detour around the dung. With youthful resolve, I was determined to complete the job I had begun, bear or not. There couldn't be that many breaks left, I told myself. Besides that, I thought, "I'm on a roll."

It was then that we came upon a second warning. There in the mud of a trailside seep were the unmistakable tracks of a good-sized grizzly. Red stopped, then nervously sidled toward the edge of the path. Each imprint was a good sixteen inches long. A part of me sounded the alarm, "Dangerous. This is way too dangerous. Get out of here, now!" I paused for several minutes. From my vantage point in the saddle, I sat scanning my surroundings. Nothing moved. Nothing seemed out of the ordinary. Vaguely encouraged, I decided to move on, keenly alert for further signs that danger could be nearby.

With the distinct possibility of startling a big bruin, I decided to make my presence known. "Hey, bear." I bellowed my greeting every few seconds as Red slowly climbed the steep trail. I recalled that one of the first rules of bear etiquette is to avoid surprising one on the trail, at all costs. This would be particularly true of a grizzly. The belief held that noises, such as calling out or singing, often averted unexpected confrontations with the powerful beasts. This theory drew on the knowledge that a forewarned bear often left the trail by choice, preferring to avoid contact with humans. As my nervous calls broke the air, I hoped the experts were right.

We moved upwards through low-growing, wind-battered pines. Red carefully picked his way along the steep, rocky trail. Next, more bear scat on the trail removed all doubt that the bruin in question had to be nearby. With senses heightened, I dismounted. Warily, I glanced about as I spliced two more small breaks in the system. Relieved, I told myself the line work was finished at last.

Only one lone task remained; testing the phone at the lookout tower by attempting a call to the ranger station. I was fairly certain that all my efforts had been successful, but the phone call would be the acid test. At that point, all I wanted to do was complete that call and get off the mountain. The wind picked up and it grew darker and colder as we made our way upward. Continually scanning our surroundings, Red and I plodded up the last series of switchbacks. Distant thunder struck a note of fear. Lightning strikes were a distinct possibility on these exposed ridges. "The lookout surely couldn't be far," I told myself. Reassurance became more difficult as the moments passed.

Nothing in my young life could have prepared me for what happened next. As Red and I rounded one of the last switchbacks, a sudden blast of wind caught my wide-brimmed hat catapulting it into the air. Before I realized what was happening, the horse spooked as the hat flew past him. As Red reared up in fright, he lost his balance in the unstable scree or small broken rock. In the explosion of that one fluid motion, I was thrown violently from the saddle. Earth and sky tumbled in confusion as I plummeted down the steep slope. The dark image of Red falling toward me caught the corner of my eye as I landed on my back with a jarring thud. Stunned, I lay there motionless. In a horrifying moment, frozen in time, the horse rolled over me. Surprise and uncertainty swept through me. Finally, as the dust from the commotion began to clear, terror gripped me. I lay there, breathless, unable to move.

Miraculously, the large thrashing beast had failed to crush my head and torso.

Staring up at the dark sky, I winced at the thought of what might happen next. The sudden violence of the event made it difficult to comprehend where I was or what had happened. Moments passed and I slowly regained my breath. Next, I was briefly aware of a clattering sound moving toward me. I slowly turned my head to see a blurry image of Red. Stopping a few feet from me, he pawed at the scree, whinnied and then walked away, reins dangling from his head. Amazingly, his saddle was still in place. I watched helplessly as he slowly picked his way down the steep trail, eventually disappearing from sight around a bend.

Still frightened and unsteady from the experience, I lay there beside the trail for several minutes. When my head had cleared a bit, I sat up. Cautiously looking about, I spied my glasses a few feet away. I reached over and picked them up. To my relief, they were

Loading up at the Belly River Ranger Station.

scratched but still in one piece. This near-sighted fireguard would have been in further trouble still, without his glasses. Peering through the scarred lenses, I immediately scanned the nearby horizons for bear. I seemed to be alone.

My jeans were torn and bloodied in places. I carefully moved each leg, neither of which appeared to be broken. Cautiously, I pulled up each pant leg and found only minor cuts and scrapes. Apparently, the loose scree had given way, cushioning me when the horse had rolled over my legs, a bit of luck that had surely spared me serious injury. I stood up and tested my limbs. Although moving was painful, I found that I could still walk. Relief swept over me as I realized that I was surely one very lucky young man.

The patter of light rain on my face quickly brought me back to reality. It was time to move on. Just a few feet off the trail, I found my green backpack lying against a pile of rocks. It must have been hurled from a saddle tie-down during the mêlée. I was filled with elation as I surveyed its contents: a dented canteen still full of water, sandwiches, and my rain poncho. In spite of my plight, a measure of good fortune was apparently still with me.

Shivering in the driving rain, I quickly donned my parka and slung the backpack over my shoulder. Now afoot, I continued my trek up the trail at a rapid pace. Just ahead, I spotted the lookout, silhouetted as a dark mass at the edge of a nearby ridge. Again, I warily scanned the misty slopes about me. No sign of life. "I'm on my own now. I've got to get myself out of this one," I thought.

As I slogged on in the rain, I began to wonder if Red had escaped injury from his rollover. Would he run into Mr. Bruin? What would Joe Heimes have to say about my lapse in common sense? In retrospect, I realized that I should have quit work and headed home at first sight of bear sign. The remainder of the job could have easily waited for another day. Also, it occurred to me that a seasoned veteran would have walked his horse up the switchbacks to the lookout rather than riding. I realized that Heimes had trained his animals to head for home if their reins were dropped. I could only hope that this training had stuck for old Red. What a mess I'd gotten him into.

It was 7:00 P.M. as I wearily made my way up the stairs to the looming tower's overlook deck. Once inside, I quickly found the phone receiver. I cranked the bell with three short rings, the call sequence to the ranger station. No response. Several more times, I went through the ritual. Self-doubt slowly began to creep over me. Had I missed a break in the phone line? I knew Heimes was always in the Ranger Station by nightfall. Frustration grew as the moments passed. Where did this leave me?

Storm clouds descended over the lookout as sheets of wind-driven rain pelted the windows. The horizon, then nearby cliffs, disappeared as a dense fog moved in. Impatiently, I paused, standing there in uncertainty. Finally, I gave the phone one last vigorous ring. To my great relief, over a static-filled line came the gravelly voice of Joe Heimes. Never was I happier to hear a simple hello. "Congratulations on fixing the phone line," he growled. He paused and then barked, "How'd you lose your horse?"

There was dead silence for a moment as I pondered my reply. Finally, I said, "You mean Red made it back?"

Heimes replied, "Oh yeah, he showed up at the corral a few minutes ago. He's scraped up a bit, nothing serious though." Another pause, then he asked, "You all right?"

In a voice thick with embarrassment, I mumbled, "Yeah, I guess so."

He mused, "So what's your story? You must've made some pretty dumb mistakes up there."

Sheepishly, I responded, "Yeah, guess I did." Then I quickly added, "I learned a lot today, though." I proceeded to explain the day's events to the seasoned old fellow.

Heimes listened intently, but in typical fashion, he retained his tough guy image. With a hoarse chuckle he said, "I'm glad you're O.K., 'cause I really didn't want to come a-looking for you in this weather. There surely is a bunch of ways to find trouble in this country." He added, "I'm glad to see you're figuring some of this out." Before ringing off, he suggested that I stay put and spend the rest of the night in the shelter of the lookout. No argument from my end of the line.

As we were nearing the end of our conversation, he sighed, "So you want me to ride up and bring your horse along in the morning or do you want to walk out?"

With no hesitation, I responded, "I'll hike out. I really don't want to get on a horse again for a while." To reassure him, I added, "I'll be there by work time." As gusty winds rattled the large window panes, our conversation drew to a close. I felt very fortunate to have a dry place to spend the stormy night. I unrolled a sleeping bag on an aged army cot. Crawling into it, I immediately lapsed into a deep sleep. It had been quite a day, one I'd long remember.

Descending the stairs of the lookout at daybreak the following morning, I watched as the first rays of the rising sun bathed Bear Mountain in a warm glow. Although a bit stiff and sore, my frame began to loosen up as I made my way down the trail. Indeed, it had dawned a beautiful day and, best of all, there was no recent sign of bear.

Within a few days, I had regained my confidence and once again mounted Red for a trip to Elizabeth Lake. After a few days afoot, it felt good to be back in the saddle again. He must have forgiven me as he made no objection to having me astride him. During my lunch break, I was able to catch and dress a limit of beautiful arctic grayling from the lake's pristine waters. The sun warmed my shoulders as we ambled back to the ranger station late that summer afternoon. In that one crystalline moment in time, I felt certain that I had the greatest job on earth.

Joe Heimes retired from the National Park Service a few years later. During his twenty-six years at the remote outpost, Heimes became a special part of the park's rich history. His winter snowshoe patrols, the renowned capture of poacher, Joe Cosley, and his undeniable backcountry skills made him a legend.

The Belly River Ranger Station is now manned by seasonal rangers during the summer months. Hi-tech phones and powerful digital radio systems have taken the place of the park's old communication setup and the often-problematic vacuum tube radios. Remnants of the park's antiquated General Electric crank telephone system are now museum pieces.

In a constant state of disrepair, the Bear Mountain Fire Lookout was eventually dismantled and removed.

15
TREED BY A GRIZ

We clung desperately to tree trunks as the bellowing grizzly ripped at the bark just below our feet. As if patrolling his prisoners, the massive animal ran wildly back and forth between us. Suddenly, he stopped and looked up, his beady black eyes fixed on my brother. Then, emitting a primeval moan, the bear raced the short distance to the tree I had climbed. Far below me, the bruin ripped at the trunk, angrily shredding it as far as he could reach. The sudden encounter was only the beginning of a long and desperate ordeal.

Visitors to our backwoods outpost were few and I'd greatly enjoyed my brother Monty's company that week. By day, he'd helped me with my park service duties and, after work, we did what we loved best; we fished. At age fifteen, Monty was just three years my junior. Together, we'd spent every summer we could remember, growing up in Glacier. The long hours of sunlight in July provided by this northern latitude allowed us coveted evening angling time. There was nothing more exciting than casting in this alpine setting…or so we thought.

Monty would hike out the next day. This evening would be our last chance to fish together for some time to come. Eagerly, I wrapped up my final fireguard duties for the day. Grabbing a quick sandwich along with our gear, we headed out. The winding path we chose followed the general course of the Belly River. It wound its way through forested slopes for two miles, at last ending at our chosen site, Dawn Mist Falls.

The beautiful white cascade of water plummeted downward into a deep, foaming pool. We couldn't get our poles rigged up quickly enough. The fine mist of the falls quickly dampened our clothes.

No matter, we were fishing. For the next hour, we were immersed in an angler's paradise. Alternately, we took turns catching and releasing several nice arctic grayling and a few smaller rainbow trout. The ultimate were two rainbows, each weighing around three pounds. These would be our keepers. Quickly dressing the fish, we donned our packs and began the short hike back to the ranger station. Imagining how good fresh trout and fried potatoes were going to taste, we headed out at a good pace down the trail.

Suddenly, a foreboding sound split the air, echoing off a bluff nearby. Instinctively, we froze in our tracks. Listening intently, Monty muttered, "What was that?" A strange silence filled the forest. The usual sounds of birds and other animals ceased. As we listened intently, only the whisper of the pines and the murmur of the quaking aspen broke the silent void. After a few moments, I shook my head and whispered, "Monty. I don't like this." We stood, back to back, scanning the landscape in all directions.

At last, Monty whispered, "There it is again. Hear it? Can you hear it?" Through the silent forest echoed a primeval wail.

My words came out in a breathless rush, "I think we're in trouble, Monty." No sooner had the words escaped me than a large, light brown object crested a nearby hill hurtling straight toward us. Still several hundred feet away, it was moving with lightning speed and closing rapidly. Monty yelled, "Grizzly!" Instinctively, we ran from the trail. Shedding our packs and fishing poles, we began to climb two nearby pines. Since the trees had no weight-bearing branches for the first thirty-five feet or so, we had no choice but to shinny. The first fifteen feet passed in a blur. No conscious thought propelled us upward, but rather the simple instinctive urge for survival.

My next lucid memory was a large bear bellowing at the base of my tree. A quick glance downward told me I needed to climb higher. Still higher. The bruin stood on his hind legs, clawing the bark just a few feet below me. Numb with fear, I poured all of my concentration into moving upward, resisting the temptation to look down. At the time, I was unaware of the stubby, dead branches that tore at my clothing and skin with each upward thrust of my body. A safe haven was all that mattered to me.

At some point, sheer exhaustion put a halt to my progress. As I clung there, struggling for breath, I could hear Monty calling, "Mark, Mark." Then, "I'm over here." I swung my head toward the sound and spied my brother in a tree, some twenty-five feet to my left. With perspiration blurring my vision, I caught the ghostly image of the animal slamming against the tree he'd climbed. Standing on his hind legs, the grizzly again furiously ripped off pieces of bark with its long, light-colored claws. Shouting encouragement, I yelled, "Hang on, Monty, just hang on!" Apparently following the sound of my voice, the large bear turned and sprinted in my direction.

With ears laid back and hair standing on end, the infuriated animal continued to race back and forth between our trees. A prominent hump atop the bear's shoulders helped confirm his identity as a grizzly rather than a large black bear. The massive beast's speed and agility belied its size. The unsettling sound it emitted was unlike anything I'd ever heard. It was, at once, both unearthly and yet indescribably chilling. After several minutes, the angry bear began to methodically shred our fishing packs. All too soon, we realized it had consumed our precious catch. We cringed as the razor sharp teeth bit our fishing poles into small pieces. Clinging to our lofty perches, we had no choice but to watch in fear and amazement as the grizzly continued his rampage.

As though they had a will of their own, our limbs trembled as muscle fatigue, at last, began to take its toll. Our only comfort was in being, temporarily, at least, out of the bruin's grasp. Moments dragged on and eventually, with a tone of desperation in his voice, Monty called out, "Mark, what's with this bear? What are we going to do?"

I responded, "I don't know. I just don't know." We'd run into the occasional grizzly bear during our previous summers in the park, but never had we encountered anything like this. We shuddered as we pondered our almost certain fate had we not had time to climb trees.

Finally, his frenzy spent, a calmer bear emitted a throaty growl and began a slow waddle away from us. The relatively open forest allowed us to watch his movements from our vantage points. Monty spoke. "I think he's leaving." Squinting in the bear's direction, he added, "Yeah, he's headed out."

I responded, "I sure hope so, because I don't think I can hang on much longer." Now about three-hundred feet away, the grizzly was hidden from my view behind a large clump of bushes.

The bear, however, was still partially visible to Monty. "Oh no," he exclaimed. "You're not going to believe this. He's not leaving at all. He's just lying there watching us." An eerie shiver ran through my body. We waited patiently. Some fifteen minutes had passed since our original encounter with the beast.

Now quiet, the animal lay in wait, watching our every move, much like a predator stalking its prey. Hope and elation were quickly replaced once more by fear and uncertainty. What to do? There seemed to be no easy solution to our predicament. It was apparent that the bear was prepared to wait us out. We realized that our best bet was to shinny up further into the trees in search of the more supportive branches. Moving cautiously and ever mindful of the consequences of a fall, we slowly inched upward. Resting often, we worked our way some fifteen feet higher into the trees' upper reaches. Although the limbs were still small and somewhat flimsy, we found that by straddling a branch, we could help support our weight by hanging onto the branches above with our arms. Though not very substantial, the flexible branches gave our shaky limbs a chance to rest and recover.

Surveying the benefits of our new positions, I shouted, "Monty! What's the bear doing?" He responded, "I don't know, can't really see him from here." Neither of us had a clear view of the bear or his bushy shelter through the dense cluster of pine needles surrounding us. Being the stronger climber, Monty volunteered to slide down to check on his whereabouts occasionally, then shinny back up into the haven of branches. It was now 8:00 P.M. As the sun slowly slipped behind the alpine peaks, it cast ever-lengthening shadows on the valley below. We began to shiver. Our torn blue jeans and tee shirts would provide little protection against the cold of the rapidly approaching night hours. The mosquitoes had found us as well. The blood from our cuts and abrasions became the ultimate attraction for the pesky insects as they descended upon us in a black haze.

Dawn Mist Falls on the Belly River.

As the nine o'clock hour came and went, Monty slid down the tree for yet another check on the bear. Dejectedly, he yelled back, "He's still there!" Again, he climbed up to the relative safety of the larger branches. It grew colder as dense gray clouds drifted in over Belly River country. With an approaching storm and the impending darkness, we found our chances for escape rapidly deteriorating. We were aware that only two hours of daylight remained before the cold night descended. While we were only a mile from the ranger station, the chances of anyone passing by on the nearby trail at this hour were extremely remote. My boss knew we were going fishing, but he had no idea of our destination. Search efforts probably wouldn't begin until the next morning and no one would have a clue where to look.

We were, quite literally, on our own, held at bay by a predator who showed no signs of giving up his watch. If darkness fell and the bear was still lying in wait for us, we had two choices: Make a stealthy descent down our trees with an attempt to sneak away down the trail; or, wait out the grizzly and attempt to survive the night hours hanging from our perches high above the forest floor.

Undoubtedly, the only sane choice was to remain within the safety of the pines. We knew it would be folly to return to the trail; the griz would be on us in an instant. It seemed we were part of a deadly cat and mouse waiting game. We were, quite clearly, the prey in the situation.

Our survival plan was risky at best. If the bear was still nearby by 10:30 P.M., we would be compelled to use the last minutes of fading light to prepare for a night-long vigil in the treetops. With our jackets and packs torn apart and scattered below us, we had only the clothes on our backs. Luckily, the knives we'd used to clean our fish were still in our pockets. With any luck, we'd be able to cut off our jeans at the knees and tear the lower portion into strips. Next, we'd planned to tie the strips together into sections long enough to lash our bodies to the tree trunks for the night. This measure would insure that if we fell asleep or if the cold became intense enough to dull our senses, we wouldn't tumble down. The nighttime temperatures had been dropping down into the high thirties. Hypothermia could well finish us off before dawn. Pondering our options, Monty murmured, "Not much of a plan is it?"

Thunder echoed off the mountain peaks to the west as a cool breeze began to sift through the lodgepole pines. The trees swayed noticeably in the face of an approaching storm. My thoughts drifted longingly to better times in my snug fireguard cabin. Next, a crescendo of thunder was rapidly followed by a heavy, driving rain. Water began dripping down from branches overhead, soaking us. We sipped at the refreshing rivulets as they made their way past us down the tree trunks.

Then, thirty minutes after it had arrived, the rainfall turned to light mist, eventually stopping altogether. The skies lightened somewhat as the cloud cover moved toward the east. As is common after a thunderstorm in Glacier, the temperature dropped noticeably. Drenched as we were, we both began to shiver uncontrollably. I called to Monty, "How you doing over there?"

There was a long silence after which he murmured, "Cold, so cold." The dejected tone in his voice mirrored my feelings exactly. We were in deep trouble. We also knew the next move was not likely to be ours.

Just as Monty prepared to slide down the tree for another visual check on our nemesis, the silence was broken by a woofing sound. There he was. The grizzly was back, peering up at us. Our hearts sank. How we had hoped that he might have moved on by now. Words weren't necessary to convey our dismay. Monty shook his head and looked away. Pressing my forehead against the tree, I closed my eyes. Several more minutes passed.

Suddenly, Monty shouted, "Look, Mark!"

I turned and watched as the grizzly slowly ambled away from our refuge in the pines. "Yeah, I see him." I called back with guarded elation. Could the bear be leaving the area for good or was this another deception? He stopped once, looked back, and then ambled over a small rise. Now, some hundred yards distant, the beast rose up on his hind legs, glanced in our direction one last time then plodded up a long slope, disappearing in the dusk.

Breathless, we waited. Five minutes passed. Could our ordeal actually be at an end? Excitedly, we made plans for a hasty escape. Our scattered fishing gear appeared to be ruined. We wouldn't waste valuable time reclaiming it as we left the scene. It was well past 10:30 P.M., and total darkness would soon be upon us. For three hours, our lives had hung in the balance. At this point, it was safe to say our only desire was to put this nightmare behind us.

Cold and sore, we made our way to the ground. The same jagged branches that tore at our bodies during our initial ascent, once again ripped at our clothing and skin. Slowly, at first, we willed our stiff limbs to carry us down the trail. Eventually, reaching a steady pace, we nervously looked back at intervals. Every sound and movement from within the shrouded forest was suspect. For all we knew, the predator could be right there pacing us in our retreat. A partial moon cast dim shadows across the forest floor. In silhouette, each tree, each shrub, windfall or boulder became a bear, poised to strike.

Profound fatigue and the mental stresses of the traumatic experience had become too much for us; we were hallucinating. Shadowy forms seemed to move along beside us in the twilight. At one point, Monty saw people on the trail ahead. We sprinted forward to catch them. They vanished into thin air before his eyes. We stood there, confused, staring about us. Our pace quickened again as total darkness overtook us.

Suddenly, we stopped dead in our tracks as a loud crack came from a nearby thicket. Our hearts pounded. We listened intently, our eyes searching the darkness in the direction of the noise. Silence. We stood motionless as another minute passed. Only the sound of a distant owl broke the stillness. Momentarily relieved, we set out running. Twice, we lost the trail and ran into the woods, tripping over windfalls and running into trees. Instinctively, we found the narrow track, with little more than the clap of our footsteps on the packed earth to guide us.

With no concept of time, we occasionally slowed and caught our breath, only to sprint away again into the darkness when we felt ready. Finally, in the distance, we heard the faint, uneven drone of the ranger station generator. The distant thrum, thrum spurred us on. The end of our journey was finally within sight. As we broke free of the forest, a light beckoned to us-a guiding beacon. Emotion rose like a giant wave in our parched throats. Sobbing tears of joy, we raced the final distance to the station.

Joe Heimes, my boss and the area ranger, opened the door in answer to our pounding fists. His jaw dropped when he spied our pale faces and torn, blood stained clothing. Bidding us to enter, he cried, "Good Lord. What happened here?" We caught our breath. Heimes disappeared into his living room. He returned with water and a first aid kit. Peering over his reading glasses intently, he commanded, "Now, sit down and tell me what happened, and I'll check these scrapes." As our story unfolded, the park veteran periodically shook his head. "Ouch!" I cried, responding to the sting of the Mercurochrome.

As we satisfied our considerable thirst, Heimes finished tending our wounds. He determined they were superficial and wouldn't need further treatment. We learned that, when we failed to return, he had alerted the trail crew. They were to begin a general search around all nearby water courses at sunup. A rather large male bear had been seen a few days earlier near where they had been working. Perhaps, because of their number, the bear made the decision to retreat.

"Damn strange bear, I'd say. Can't imagine why he didn't leave the area. You'd think that he'd let you be after he ate your fish." Then with typical Heimes humor, he mused, "You know, it's illegal to feed the bears in the park." It was midnight when we left the ranger station and made the short trek to my fireguard cabin. Sleep found us quickly.

Monty bade me goodbye and left early the next morning, heading in the opposite direction of our previous day's adventure. It wouldn't take him long to reach civilization. To my dismay, Heimes announced that we'd abandon our customary work schedule and head out to the site of our encounter with the grizzly. I wanted no part of the return trip, but Heimes was the boss and he wanted to monitor the incident area. Besides, someone needed to pick up the remnants of our fishing gear. Mounting our horses, we slowly left the safe environs of the ranger station turning onto the main trail.

As we rode along, my confidence slowly returned. Heimes was a skilled marksman and the fact that he carried two Remington .30-06 rifles in saddle scabbards definitely helped to ease my concerns.

At last I called out, "There, over there." We brought our horses to an abrupt halt and dismounted. Heimes pulled both rifles from their holsters, motioning for me to take one. He quickly reviewed the workings of the firing mechanism and how to hold the rifle in firing position. Somewhat apologetically, I assured him that my father had taught me how to use a similar rifle.

"No matter," he said, "I still don't want you pointing that thing anywhere near me. It's loaded, you know. The last thing I need is to be shot by a greenhorn kid." Then, in a hoarse voice he said, "Now show me exactly where all this took place." I pointed out the two distant pines in which the grizzly had treed us. As we moved forward, I motioned toward a patch of shrubbery and whispered, "That's where the bear waited for us." Ahead, just off of the trail, lay the scattered remains of our fishing gear.

In hushed tones, Heimes ordered me to keep a sharp lookout. With rifles shouldered, we slowly edged forward. Maintaining a safe distance, we carefully maneuvered around the shrubs. There seemed to be no sign of the bear. A keen sense of relief swept over me. The events of the previous night still lingered indelibly in my mind.

"Oh my," said Heimes, "Would you look at that?" He pointed toward a mutilated carcass. Still vigilant, we drew closer and examined the remains. A crushed skull, miscellaneous bones, and a portion of the hide were all that were left of the unfortunate creature. "Yep, that was a deer," mumbled Heimes. "Those holes in its skull sure look like they were made by the canine teeth of a grizzly." Next to the carcass was a good sized depression in the soft mantle of pine needles that covered the forest floor. He pointed, exclaiming, "Right there's where your bear was lying."

The mystery of the grizzly's staying power was now becoming

clear. Heimes surmised that our appearance on the trail the previous day had ventured too close to the bear's food source. He was, undoubtedly, protecting his carcass and the territory around it. As we hung from our nearby trees, the bear viewed us both as a threat and a nuisance. The trout in our fishing packs must have presented an enticing snack.

Heimes cast a disapproving glance at our shredded fishing gear and laughed, "Now just look at this mess here. You've gone and broken another law. Don't you know that it's illegal to litter in the park?" One pack, a fishing reel and a canteen were the only items worth salvaging. Judging by the damage, he said, "Yep, I'd say you were pretty lucky here, young fellow. Let's pack this stuff up and head back home. Your bear is probably long gone." He added, "You never know about a grizzly. I don't reckon that we'll ever really figure them out." As if to heighten the mystique, the bear wasn't seen again that summer.

Monty and I continued to live and work in Glacier for many seasons to come. In later years, we often revisited the fishing spots of our youth. We saw grizzlies from time to time and occasionally met them on the trail, but neither of us ever had an aggressive encounter again. Still, we maintain that unpredictability is perhaps the most distinguishing trait of the grizzly...the hallmark of an animal seldom understood.

We were very lucky to have survived our encounter with the great bear that July 18, 1959. Sadly, on precisely the same date the following summer, our younger brother, Smitty, and fellow hikers would be involved in a horrific attack by a female grizzly.

16

THE OTOKOMI GRIZZLY
BEAR ATTACK

July 1960 - Mark and Smitty Parratt – Otokomi Lake Trail

Author's Note: The summer of 1960 would tragically and permanently alter the lives of our family and the closely knit group of fellow park service workers whose friendships we shared. Our father, Lloyd Parratt, was stationed at the Saint Mary headquarters as lead seasonal ranger naturalist that summer. My youngest brother, Smitty, lived with our parents in the park housing complex near the ranger station. At age ten, Smitty was an eager participant in all hiking and outdoor activities that presented themselves. The stunning beauty of Glacier Park's alpine terrain was irresistible to hikers and climbers alike during those long summer days. Now, many decades later, the story of the Otokomi Grizzly Bear Attack still brings tears to my eyes. This account is written from my own perspective. The passages that appear in italics were written by Smitty, one of the unfortunate victims of the attack.

As a fireguard at Many Glacier Ranger Station, I was enjoying my second summer as an employee of the National Park Service. Working with Area Ranger Larry Dale, I was given the responsibilities of maintaining an aged Jeep fire truck as well as tending a small fire cache. I also worked as a member of the area's search and rescue team. It was mid-July and our group had already been involved in hiking and climbing rescues within the park.

From a very young age, I was enthralled with adventure and rarely passed up an opportunity to join friends hiking the mountain trails. This day was no exception. It was a chance to see new backcountry, breathe hard and enjoy the beauty of Glacier's wilderness.

High in the backcountry of Glacier National Park lies a spectacular jewel known as Otokomi Lake. Reached by a trailhead which departs from Rising Sun Campground in Saint Mary valley, its remote waters are seldom frequented by park visitors.

On July 18, 1960, a small hiking party spent most of the day fishing Otokomi's pristine depths. By late afternoon, their creels still empty, the group made the decision to begin their trek homeward. Smitty had begged to accompany Alan Nelson and Ed Mazzer, park service ranger naturalists, on the day hike. Joining the trio on the trail were Swedish tourists, Brita Noring and Gote Nyhlen.

At a gathering the evening before the outing, Nelson and Mazzer debated the safety of hiking in the vicinity of Otokomi Lake. One week earlier, park visitor, Tom Shea, had been attacked on the Otokomi trail by a large female grizzly bear. Violating park policy, Shea brought his dog on the hike. It was the general consensus of the park community that the animal's barks may have agitated the grizzly, provoking the attack. Justifying their hike, Mazzer and Nelson rationalized the bear and her cubs would likely have moved out of the Otokomi valley after a week's time.

Still, a feeling of uneasiness hung in the air late that afternoon as the small group left the placid alpine setting of Otokomi Lake. They followed a steep, rocky trail that passed through dense patches of alder and willow brush. A premonition of impending disaster seemed to grow more intense as the group proceeded down the track. Wariness overtook them. They slowed their pace.

Suddenly, I was overwhelmed by a sense of intense anxiety. I felt, with certainty, that we were going to be attacked by a grizzly bear. Although we had not seen evidence to suggest the presence of a bear, we all suspected one could be nearby. I spoke to Nelson, "Alan, do you think we are going to be attacked by a bear?"

He responded, "Shhh." I could see the fear that was written across his face... the same look of concern mirrored by the others.

About a mile below Otokomi Lake, the group fell into single file as the trail narrowed. Smitty cautiously moved to the rear of the line. With Mazzer now in the lead, they picked their way down the steep path which was surrounded by thickets of subalpine fir. Now, with a rapid drop in elevation, the hikers passed through a meadow, then into the dense forest once again.

Meanwhile, nearby, a female grizzly and her two cubs slowly ambled in the direction of the trail. The mother stopped to feed on succulent corn lily bulbs as her playful young tussled with one another at her side.

Slightly ahead of the group, Mazzer rounded a bend in the trail. He stopped abruptly. Fear washed over the naturalist as he caught sight of the sow and cubs moving up the trail toward him. He turned quickly and raced back up the trail to warn his companions. With beady eyes focused on the fleeing hiker, the mother grizzly quickly closed the distance between them. Glimpsing the enraged bear hurtling toward him, Mazzer quickly climbed to safety in a nearby fir.

His shouts initially confused the Swedish tourists. However, quick to follow his lead, they reached trees and began to climb.

Ed screamed, "Grizzly. Run for your lives!" The group scattered in terror. My parents had drummed into my head never to run from a grizzly. So there I stood as my four companions ran for the trees.

I quickly glanced down the trail at the gigantic grizzly bear churning straight toward me. The sound of the rasping, deep, guttural grunt that accompanied each stride sent waves of panic through my body. Then, when perhaps half the original distance was consumed, I, too, fled. I ran like the wind, dodging bushes and leaping over downed trees.

Nelson and Smitty headed for a grove of evergreens on the far side of the trail. The grizzly was closing fast. As they neared the trees, the bear reached Smitty, pouncing on him and knocking him to the ground. Nelson glanced back, horrified to see the boy picked up and tossed about by the powerful creature. As the grizzly chewed and clawed, flesh was torn from the back of Smitty's head. His face was raked by the massive claws.

Despite my best effort to evade the bear, she caught up to me very quickly. I can only remember bits and pieces of the next few moments, as I was thrown high into the air. I felt helpless as the bear's jaws repeatedly closed on the back of my head, tearing off my scalp. Oddly enough, I was unaware of the damage as it occurred to my face, chest and arm. I was completely at the mercy of the grizzly's attack.

Now, standing behind a tree, Nelson began to shout at the furious bear to distract her from his young friend. The creature spun around and immediately charged the man. In desperation, he wheeled about, and attempted to climb a nearby tree. As he struggled upward, dead branches broke off in his hands, dropping him toward the growling bear. Now, the enraged sow reared up, grabbed him by his buttocks and pulled him down from the tree. Nelson screamed as he slammed into the forest floor, face first. "I'm dead," he thought.

He felt the beast moving over his body and would long remember the grunting sounds and the foul breath of the animal as it hovered above him. The bear used her long claws and snout repeatedly as she attempted to turn him over onto his back. Spreading his arms and legs to gain leverage and grasping vegetation, Nelson summoned all his remaining strength to thwart her efforts. He knew that his best chance for survival hinged upon remaining face down and playing dead. Again and again, the bear inflicted deep bites to the backs of his thighs.

Suddenly, the animal ceased her attack on Nelson and turned toward sounds coming from the opposite side of the trail.

Brita stood at the base of the pine tree where Gote had found refuge. Catching sight of the woman, the bear charged in her direction. Upon reaching Brita, it reared up on its hind legs. With its lips curled back in a menacing snarl, hairs bristling on its telltale grizzly hump, the bear now stood, face to face with the woman. Consumed with fear, she froze and remained motionless for several moments. Finally, the bear dropped to all fours and began to move away.

At this point, clinging to a branch in the pine where he had taken refuge, Gote saw his chance. He reached down to his companion. In a hoarse whisper, he urged, "Climb, Brita, climb!" Grasping his

This picture of the female grizzly was taken from Ed Mazzer's position in the tree and retouched by the FBI.

outstretched hand, his friend struggled up. Moments before she could reach safety, the bear lunged up toward her, crushed her ankle in its mouth, then dragged her from the tree.

Lying injured nearby, Nelson could only listen as the bear savagely attacked the screaming woman. The beast tore at her side repeatedly, laying flesh bare. Next, the bear grabbed her leg in its powerful jaws, dragging her into the underbrush. The beast abandoned her momentarily. Then suddenly, the sow returned, and in a final gesture, aggressively bit her arm.

The grizzly finally left Noring and returned to the other two victims who lay injured on the ground. Both were conscious, yet remained motionless as the great bear hovered over them watching for signs of life. Nelson could feel the heat of the animal's breath on the back of his neck and thought, "Oh, no, here we go again."

Ed Mazzer and Gote Nyhlen had both climbed trees, where they clung, safe from the bear's reach. The frightened pair shouted in repeated attempts to distract the animal as they watched her fearsome assault on their three companions.

After the bear left me, time drifted aimlessly. Although I was aware of my surroundings, the events that followed seemed to play out in a detached fashion. I felt no pain and my fear had vanished. As the minutes dragged on, I began to explore the extent of my injuries, first discovering the opening in my side. With each breath, air made a hissing sound as it escaped from my punctured lung. I felt about me and found a nearby leaf that worked fairly well to block the air leak. The bone from my right upper arm protruded from the flesh an inch or so. It alarmed me to feel its jagged edge. Next, came the stark realization that I couldn't see. Both of my eyes had been pulled from their sockets. Moments later, I found that if I lifted one eye from where it rested on my cheek, a tiny fraction of my surroundings came into view. Realizing the gravity of my injuries, I felt a deep sense of loneliness and wanted, more than anything, to be near another human being.

Nelson lay prostrate on the ground. Following the attack, arms covering his head, he listened for the bear. At last, he glanced over his shoulder, in order to survey the extent of his injuries. In disbelief, he recoiled at the sight of the blood bath about his legs. He made the decision not to stand, fearing he could bleed to death.

Suddenly, Nelson became aware of soft cries drifting across the meadow. Recognizing Smitty's voice, he called back to the young boy. At last, each had found a human connection.

Hearing Nelson's calls, I rose up out of my timeless drifting long enough to take a course of action. Using the tiny square of my vision that remained and guided by Alan's calls, I rose. Cradling my broken arm, I slowly made my way to where he lay, at the foot of a tree. As I approached him, I recall his shocked expression. He blurted out, "Oh, my God." At his direction, I nestled close to him. He covered me with his jacket and peace came at last with the knowledge that I would not be alone when I died.

Blood oozing from open wounds soon attracted swarms of mosquitoes to the pair. Nelson found that covering their injuries with clothing was the only way to keep the hungry insects at bay.

Meanwhile, from their vantage points in nearby trees, Mazzer and Nyhlen watched and waited. After some thirty minutes, the sow and her cubs wandered from view. Eventually, convinced the bears had left the area, the two men cautiously made their way to the ground.

They soon found their way to where Nelson and young Smitty lay. It was readily apparent that both were gravely injured and in deep shock. Warily scanning their surroundings, the men attempted to comfort their companions. A quick search of the surrounding area showed no trace of the Swedish woman. Where was she? The winds sifting through the pines offered no clues.

A sense of reality slowly began to replace the emotions of shock and disbelief. Both men realized a concerted rescue effort was called for, to save the lives of the injured. Mazzer trembled as he huddled over the bloodied body of his colleague. His voice quavered, "What should we do, Alan? That grizzly can't be far away." He glanced about nervously. "We need to get help up here...fast." After a deep sigh, he breathed, "My God, I can't believe this."

Following a brief discussion, it was decided that first Mazzer, then Nyhlen, would hike out to seek help. Reason told them to space their departures so, if the bear attacked, at least one of them might survive in order to summon aid.

So, hearts pounding, the men, each in his own time, began the steep, arduous hike down the trail to Rising Sun. Mazzer picked his way down the rocky path, casting wary glances into the forest. In his heart, he felt certain one or more of his injured companions would die before help could arrive.

A short time later, the cries of Brita Noring floated across the mountain meadow, cries that became fainter as the late afternoon shadows lengthened.

It was 6:00 P.M., nearly two hours since the attack. First, Mazzer, then Nyhlen, hurried past the Otokomi Lake trailhead into Rising Sun Campground. Arriving at Mazzer's car within minutes of one another, they sped off to summon help.

Soon, the men reached Saint Mary Ranger Station. Their vehicle screeched to a halt at the home of District Ranger James Godboldt. Hearing their approach, the ranger left his dinner table and hurried to the front door. Seeing the distraught pair, he listened intently as Mazzer blurted a hasty account of the tragedy. With a grim expression, Godboldt shook his head in disbelief, "I'll get my team together and we'll meet you at the fire cache." Pausing briefly, he called to his wife. "Barbara. Young Smith Parratt has been mauled in a grizzly attack. Would you please break the news to his parents as gently as you can?"

Reaching the fire cache's communications center, Godboldt rapidly mobilized the Saint Mary search and rescue crew. The radio crackled as his emergency alert was broadcast to all stations in the park. He voiced an urgent need for backup rescue, medical personnel and armed marksmen.

As men poured from the dormitory nearby, Godboldt quickly

planned his rescue strategy. A bear attack of this magnitude was a rarity in the history of Glacier Park. A seasoned leader, he sensed the danger this night held for the victims as well as those who set out to rescue them.

Meanwhile, in their apartment, Lloyd and Grace Parratt were enjoying a quiet dinner with friends. They had just voiced concerns that Smitty and his companions were noticeably late returning from their day's hike. In fact, an uneasy feeling had preoccupied the Parratts throughout the evening. Grace remarked, "Smitty is never late for dinner. Lloyd, I'm worried about them. You don't suppose they ran into some kind of trouble, do you?"

As if in reply, the silence was broken by an urgent knock at the front door. They arose from the table. Opening the door, they found Barbara Godboldt, her eyes wide with alarm. Speaking in hushed tones, she said, "Lloyd, could you step outside for a moment?"

Grace stood at the window, watching intently as the ranger's wife delivered the alarming news. By her husband's anguished expression, she knew misfortune had befallen their youngest son. Hastily opening the door, Lloyd turned to his wife. He held her close as he told her what had happened. After a hasty discussion, it was agreed she would remain with their dinner companions for the time being. Lloyd Parratt grabbed his jacket and rucksack and sprinted toward the fire cache.

The intense activity in the office became a blur as he glanced about. Catching sight of Ed Mazzer, he approached him. The naturalist placed his arm across Lloyd's shoulder, quickly relating the details of the grizzly attack and its aftermath. The distraught father grimaced as the brief conversation ended. Looking into Mazzer's eyes he somehow sensed the gravity of his son's injuries. An overwhelming sense of apprehension swept over him.

As a plan began to take shape in his mind, Lloyd hastily returned to the apartment where Grace stood waiting. She recognized her husband's need to join in the rescue effort. Comforted by close friends, she could only wait and pray. Ironically, a mere twenty-four hours earlier, the Parratt apartment rang with joy and laughter as the pair celebrated their twenty-third wedding anniversary.

It was 6:45 P.M., as the first Saint Mary search and rescue crew dispatched from the Otokomi trailhead. Designated as Team One, their sole purpose was to reach the scene of the attack in order to set up rescue operations. The team remained vigilant, as it was impossible to predict the location or the mindset of the grizzly. The men moved quickly up the steep incline bearing stretchers, lights and medical equipment. Preceding the group was a pair of rangers armed with high-powered rifles.

At 6:55 P.M., Dr. Lewis Reese, resident physician at Many Glacier Hotel, was notified of the bear attack. He summoned his wife, a registered nurse. Together, they quickly assembled emergency medical equipment and left in their car for Rising Sun.

A second, larger rescue crew from Saint Mary, Team Two, began its ascent at 7:00 P.M. Equipped with additional bicycle stretchers and first aid supplies, this group included Lloyd Parratt. Anxious to reach his injured son, he struggled to envision the scene that awaited him as dusk overtook the forest ahead.

The stunning news of the bear attack spread swiftly throughout the Glacier Park community. By now, a makeshift command post had taken shape at Rising Sun Campground. Surrounding the Otokomi Lake trailhead, portable lights flickered as campers brought food and blankets to aid in the rescue effort. The intensity of the unfolding drama pervaded the camp. Speaking in hushed tones, campers mingled as they awaited news of the injured. Camp stoves were set up on picnic tables as volunteers stepped forward to prepare food.

And now I felt the certainty of my impending death, which seemed to descend upon me like the cool breezes whispering down Otokomi valley. As sure as the sun rises and sets, I knew that my life was ebbing. I was glad to feel Alan's warm body next to mine, as I did not want to die alone.

Rather than fear, I felt a deep sadness...the sorrow of being unable to say goodbye to my family. Still adrift in time, a feeling of comfort seemed to envelop me. I moved slowly down a white tunnel which I knew was the pathway to death.

In my heart, I whispered my last farewells to my family. I realized I was not in control as my life force moved down the tunnel to pause at its far end. Then, without explanation, I began to return. The mysterious journey and its pause on the brink of eternity (which may have lasted minutes or only a fraction of a second) was to change, forever, my perspectives on life and death.

I had just finished a day of testing equipment at the fire cache. The sun began to glow in the west and mountain shadows began to cast Many Glacier valley in silhouette. I asked myself, "Does life get any better than this?"

Making my way toward the trail crew bunkhouse nearby, I looked up to see ranger Larry Dale hurrying toward me. Visibly shaken, his voice was hoarse with urgency, "Mark, there's been a grizzly bear attack near Otokomi Lake. They've put out an urgent call for our search and rescue team. There were several people injured and they need our help to get them out of there."

Larry quickly assembled his Many Glacier crew. A dozen recruits grabbed their gear, and then jogged toward waiting trucks. I was among the group. Silence fell over us, as the twisting mountain highway brought us closer to the command post, some forty minutes away. In route, we learned that three hikers had been seriously mauled by a sow grizzly. Two rescue teams had already headed up the mountain.

Our group, Team Three, arrived at the base camp at 7:30 P.M. With daylight turning to dusk, we wasted no time donning our gear. It was then that a distraught Larry Dale took me aside and quietly confided, "Mark, you know a number of the injured personally. One is your brother, Smitty. I didn't want to tell you until we got here. If you choose not to go with us, I'll certainly understand. Your dad headed up with Team Two not long ago."

For one fleeting moment, my thoughts froze and my mind went blank. The surreal quality of the lighted base camp suddenly seemed like a disjointed nightmare. How could Smitty be part of this? How badly was he injured? Countless questions raced through my mind. Among them, "Who else was mauled? Are they still alive?"

As reality overtook my frightened imaginings, I realized a

response was called for. "Larry, I have no choice. That's my little brother up there."

My boss would later confess that he'd asked himself, "What would I do if a grizzly injured my brother?" My answer was no surprise to him.

As we headed up the mountain, shadows gradually closed in on the trail. The cool breezes which swept down upon us carried with them the earthy scents of lush meadow and dense forest. Breathing hard, we moved along the steep trail at a brisk pace, each man keeping a wary eye on the shadows as we passed. The group's only safety net lay in the pair of rifle-bearers who preceded it. Each sound heard from the forest became a perceived threat, bringing a temporary halt to the procession. At one point, a deer bounded through the dry forest, sending a twinge of alarm through each pounding heart. Everyone knew the female grizzly was out there somewhere, hidden by the deepening shadows.

As we trudged along, I prayed, "God, please, be with Smitty and the others up there."

Now, the steep, rocky track forced the crew to move more slowly, compounding their fear with a sense of frustration. The minutes dragged as we struggled upward.

At 8:00 P.M., Team One neared the site where Mazzer indicated the bear had attacked. With lights flickering across a tree-studded meadow, the rescue crew approached cautiously. Suddenly, a call echoed through the darkness, "Over here." A jittery lead rifleman instinctively swung his weapon toward the sound of the voice. Alan Nelson begged, "Don't shoot," adding, "Smitty and I are over here." Upon reaching the injured naturalist, the rescuers saw the small, bloodied body of the young boy lying next to him.

Next, a group of men conducted a careful search of the meadow and its periphery. They were relieved to find no sign of the grizzly or her cubs. The victims' soft moans belied the screams of terror that had shattered the solitude here some four hours earlier.

Upon hearing anguished calls from deep within the forest, they searched in vain for the third victim, Brita Noring. Walking among scattered trees, the men followed the echoes of her calls. Suddenly, as they peered into the darkness, the ground near them shuddered. Incredulously, a bloodied hand emerged from the forest floor. Brita Noring had been found. Fearing renewed attacks from the bear, she had covered her entire body with a thick carpet of earth and pine needles.

Now began the difficult task of administering first aid to the victims' deep, bone-baring gashes and shredded flesh. Rescuers winced as they struggled with compresses and bandages in the failing light. One ranger gasped, "Unbelievable." He swallowed hard, muttering, "These people need skilled trauma surgeons and they need them now!"

Seasonal ranger, Al Kytonen, arriving with Team One, was in charge of the bulky radio pack set. He calmly spoke to base camp, describing the victims' injuries. In response, a waiting Dr. Reese listened intently, then transmitted instructions. Rangers worked feverishly, applying large compression bandages to stem further blood loss.

Stretchers mounted on bicycle wheels were readied to transport the victims down the steep trail. Smitty would be carried out first.

His injuries were life-threatening and his condition grave. The two adults, both in serious condition, would be transported by additional stretcher teams shortly after Smitty's departure.

Meanwhile, Team Four, arriving from West Glacier, began its ascent. The massive rescue operation now involved some forty men on the trail. Dozens of men and women waited at the base camp.

At 8:30 P.M., Team Two from Saint Mary reached the scene of the attack. Breaking from the group, Lloyd Parratt scanned the meadow in search of his young son. He slowly approached a small figure, lying nearby, already heavily swathed in bandages. Suddenly, Al Kytonen stepped forward, effectively blocking his way. The stocky ranger seized Dad by the shoulders saying, "Lloyd, I tell you, as a father and your friend, do not look at Smitty. He isn't good." Stepping into the shadows, arms about one another, the two men prayed for the young life that was slowly ebbing, nearby.

Moments later, my group, Many Glacier's Team Three, arrived on the scene. As I stood there, a figure emerged from the darkness. I recognized my father as he approached me. We embraced, weeping, as the small figure was strapped to the first stretcher. With trembling voice, Dad repeated, "Mark, the bear got his face. He's really bad." Still clinging to one another, we sank to the ground. Dad held me tightly.

After a few moments, he arose and walked quickly to his young son's side and spoke to him. Hearing his father, Smitty responded. A weak, raspy voice implored, "Dad, please hold my hand. Don't leave me." Lloyd took his son's hand and spoke gently to him throughout the long, rocky trek to the base camp. He would later confide that he feared this would be his final journey with his son. As the stretcher crew moved slowly down the trail, every bounce sent daggers of pain through Smitty's wounds. His cries became weaker and weaker.

The young boy's condition worsened even as the men struggled with the balky stretcher. His blood pressure plummeted. His body temperature continued to drop.

The five-mile journey to the base camp seemed an eternity. Every fifteen minutes, an alternate crew stepped forward to handle the stretcher. The men spoke to each other in whispers as the cold night wore on.

Emotionally distraught, I followed the group in silence. Colleagues would occasionally move beside me on the trail saying, "Hang in there, Mark. This has to be tough…we're with you all the way."

I thought to myself, "How could anyone possibly know the pain I'm feeling?" As I struggled to clear my mind, I realized they were doing their best. Many were long time coworkers, part of our park service family. Rescue operations nearly always involved strangers, but this one posed a very different scenario for everyone.

Finally, dim lights flickered in the distance. Base camp at last. With relief, the weary men welcomed the hum of generators and the blur of activity suddenly surrounding them.

The time stood at 10:45 P.M., an agonizing seven hours since the bear's attack. Dr. Lewis Reese stood nearby, awaiting the arrival of the injured. Under the glare of bright lamps, the physician quickly assessed Smitty's extensive injuries. Lloyd watched from the shadows, reluctant to interfere with the medical team's efforts to help his son. His eyes stared blankly ahead, his face a weary ashen gray.

Smitty was moved onto another stretcher and gingerly placed into the back of a makeshift park service ambulance. He moaned softly, drifting in and out of consciousness. A ranger huddled near the small form, holding an I.V. saline drip for the long trip to the hospital. Remarkably, two tourists with compatible Type O negative blood volunteered to accompany them. As the ambulance doors closed, Dr. Reese shouted to the driver, "We're running out of time here. This boy is critical." He slapped the side of the vehicle, spouting an urgent, "Go!"

With emergency lights flashing and siren blaring, the ambulance sped off down the highway through the dark Montana night. The nearest hospital was located in Cardston, Alberta, Canada, some forty-two miles to the north.

As the taillights disappeared in the distance, Dr. Reese took Dad and me aside to offer a bleak update. His prognosis held out little hope. The physician walked away and my father brushed tears from his face saying, "Mark, I've never felt so helpless." Then, wordlessly, we climbed into the back of a waiting patrol car which took us to the Parratt apartment in Saint Mary.

Meanwhile, alerted by the park service, the emergency room at Cardston Municipal Hospital became the focal point of preparation. Sensing the magnitude of the emergency, the staff immediately summoned additional trauma surgeons from medical centers to the north. Cardston Hospital's readiness and timing could well determine the fate of the three injured Americans.

Customs Agents at the United States-Canadian border were notified of the situation. The gates at the Piegan Port of Entry, normally closed at 10:00 P.M., swung open wide for the approaching vehicles. The ambulance carrying Smitty quickly sped onto Canadian soil.

Now, lapsing into unconsciousness, the boy's breathing was labored and shallow. Bubbles of blood slowly oozed from the gauze which covered the hole in his side. A jagged rib had punctured his lung. His pulse was slow and erratic. Smitty was dying.

Back in Saint Mary, after a brief, emotional reunion at their apartment, Lloyd and Grace Parratt made their way to a friend's waiting car. Soon they were bound for the Cardston Hospital.

In the interim, I remained at my parent's apartment awaiting the arrival of my brother, Monty. Only three years my junior, he and I were as close as two brothers could be...best friends and constant childhood companions. Monty was employed that summer as a gas station attendant in nearby East Glacier.

Meanwhile, to the north, further drama played out as a Royal Canadian Mounted Policeman departed from Lethbridge, Alberta, carrying two pints of precious blood for Smitty. Driving at speeds in excess of one-hundred miles per hour, the lone police sergeant raced toward the hospital with his life-giving cargo cradled in a small box beside him. Our family was never to know the anonymous donors.

The ambulance reached the Cardston Hospital emergency entrance just before midnight. With a very weak pulse, Smitty's life was near its end. As medical personnel pushed the stretcher into the emergency room, his young heart ceased beating. Finding no radial pulse, doctors immediately seized a syringe filled with adrenaline. They plunged the long needle directly into his heart, administering the life-giving drug. Precious seconds ticked by as the surgical team waited for a heartbeat. Silence filled the room like a vacuum. Medical personnel exchanged worried glances as the moments passed. Then, a beep was finally heard on the heart monitor. Erratic at first, the sounds soon fell into a healthy rhythm. A guarded, but celebratory chorus of voices arose and activity, once again, filled the room.

Miraculously, within seconds, the policeman's car skidded to a halt near the empty ambulance. Smitty's transfusion had arrived just in time.

I have no recollection of the moment my heart ceased to beat, no memory of the extraordinary measures being used to save my life. Drifting timelessly, I had the unique experience of looking down upon my body from above. High in a corner of the room, I watched the gowned doctors and nurses working over me. Bathed in a white light my surreal view faded away as the medical team again managed to revive my motionless heart.

A short time later, ambulances arrived bearing injured ranger naturalist, Alan Nelson, and Swedish schoolteacher, Brita Noring. Three, and sometimes four, trauma surgeons labored nine hours over the three injured. One of the doctors was trained as a Canadian flight surgeon during World War II. He remarked that, not since the war, had he seen a face wound as severe as Smitty's.

The elder Parratts agonized over their young son's plight through the early hours of a new day. Sleep had not been possible for the pair. Close friends and colleagues surrounded them as they awaited news, any news, from the operating room.

The waiting room clock showed 5:00 A.M. as the head surgeon appeared in the doorway. In a weary voice, he called out, "Mr. and

Mrs. Parratt?" Speaking quietly, he motioned for the pair to step down the hall. "I am always honest about a patient's prognosis. Smitty's is not good. We had considerable difficulty stabilizing his heartbeat when he first arrived. We have completed the surgical repairs that were absolutely necessary. The shock of further surgery, at this time, could be too much for him. All we can do, now, is try to keep him stable. We feel it is doubtful that your son will survive the next twenty-four hours. If he does, he will be blind for the rest of his life. I wish I could give you more encouraging news. We've done our best. Now, it's up to the Man Upstairs." His eyes moist with emotion, he embraced each of them. Despondently, they turned and walked slowly back to the waiting room.

After briefly updating their friends, the pair followed the hospital chaplain to a room nearby. Here, they talked and prayed for nearly an hour. Numbed by their ongoing nightmare, Lloyd and Grace had gone for thirty-five hours without sleep. After finding a nearby motel, the pair slipped into a fitful slumber.

Hours later, returning to the hospital, they were given a grim update. Still uncertain if Smitty would survive, they listened as the hospital's head nurse gave an inventory of his injuries. "The left eye was torn from its socket and severed from the optic nerve. It was removed along with bone fragments from the eye socket. The right eye, which had also been torn from its socket, was surgically replaced in its moorings. We have every reason to believe he is blind at this time and we see little hope for significant change. There were severe compound fractures of the entire facial area. His scalp suffered serious lacerations and we basically had to suture it together around his skull. He has five broken ribs. As a result, his right lung was punctured and has collapsed. We've managed to repair the puncture. Smitty also has a compound fracture of his right upper arm. His condition is extremely grave. I am so very sorry. We are doing all that we can at this time to keep him stable."

Shuddering with emotion, the weary parents held one another.

Alan Nelson and Brita Noring were listed as stable and in fair condition. Nelson had sustained extensive damage to the backs of both thighs. Noring was diagnosed with severe muscle damage to her lower right leg and deep lacerations to her buttocks.

A number of park service employees from Saint Mary drove to Cardston the next morning to check on their friends, donating record quantities of blood. Over thirty-two pints were required by the victims in the first week alone.

Remaining behind at the Saint Mary apartment, my heart ached for Smitty and my beleaguered parents. I had never felt so alone, so vulnerable. Sleep eluded me as flashbacks of the previous night continuously swirled through my mind.

After forcing down a banana and a bowl of dry cereal, I walked outside and sat dejectedly on the curb. I watched the pink glow of dawn softly touch the nearby mountaintops and thought about my family, each of us hurting in his own way. There was still no word from the Cardston Hospital predicting whether Smitty would live though this new day.

Abruptly, I was jolted back to reality. A pickup truck ground to a halt nearby. Monty bolted from the cab and raced toward me. Embracing, neither of us spoke. Only the sounds of our sobs broke the silence of the still morning air.

At last, in a hoarse whisper, Monty confessed, "I thought you were the one who was attacked. No one could tell me what happened, for sure." We sat on the curb, a brotherly arm flung about each other's shoulders. Together, we agonized over whether we would ever see our young brother again. Feeling a closeness only family can share, we tried to believe that Smitty and his companions would survive. Later that morning, we headed for Cardston to join our parents.

The long summer days seemed to flow like an endless stream. Smitty began to amaze us all as time passed. The fact that he had survived was a miracle in itself. Then, ever so slowly, his condition began to improve. Mom kept a faithful watch at his bedside, catching brief naps when Smitty lapsed into fitful slumber. His head and much of his body swathed in bandages, he lay in a world of darkness, where nurses came and went, attending to his needs. Now alert, the sounds of the hospital became routine. The grinding pain slowly diminished, as healing took place.

My big day finally arrived. The doctors were to remove the bandages which had encased my head for what seemed like an eternity. This day would determine if I would be able to see. As the gauze was removed, layer by layer, faint light penetrated the dressings. Moments later, as they cleared away the last of the bandages, I regained one of my life's greatest gifts...vision.

Doctors confessed their surprise that Smitty could see with his remaining eye. One noted, "The optic nerve was badly bruised and abraded. It's remarkable that the eye actually functions." Physical and emotional healing progressed as his surgical procedures continued. Weeks passed. Smitty was continually surrounded by the love and support of family and friends.

One day I recall hearing the doctors in conversation outside my room. One of them said, "We need to cut out Smitty's antibiotics." At age ten, fearfully, I tried to imagine which internal organ the antibiotics might be. When the doctor entered my room, moments later, I begged him, "Doctor, please don't cut out my antibiotics."

Later, the family learned that Alan Nelson, the naturalist who had led the ill-fated hike, had risked death by calling the rampaging bear away from Smitty. His intervention during the attack had saved Smitty's life. Nelson noted, "The big bear kept tossing Smitty about like he was a rag doll. I knew I had to help him."

Following weeks in the hospital, Nelson and Brita Noring were well enough to be transferred to hospitals near their respective homes. After a lengthy trip by car, Nelson was hospitalized in his hometown of Bismarck, North Dakota. Here, he would spend the next two months, enduring seven painful skin grafts to his thigh. Brita Noring was flown from Calgary, Alberta, Canada, to her home in Stockholm, Sweden.

Both adults survived, but with physical and emotional scars that would last throughout their lives.

At last, Smitty was strong enough to be airlifted to a hospital near the Parratt home in Upland, California. An ambulance waited nearby on the tarmac as the turbines of the large passenger jet spooled down at the Los Angeles International Airport. Grace and Smitty were warmly greeted by attendants from the Children's Hospital of Los Angeles. They were soon transported to the renowned medical center. Here, Smitty would spend countless weeks enduring further surgical procedures.

At last, the long awaited day arrived when Smitty was released and allowed to continue his recovery at home. However, he would return to the hospital many times for extended bouts of plastic surgery. Daily lessons were provided by a home teacher. With one good eye and a strong will, he proved to be an eager student.

With his obvious disfigurement, all of his steely determination was required to brave the constant stares and questions whenever he ventured out.

Smitty returned to regular classes at Pioneer Junior High the following year. Over time, he began to excel in his school studies. In addition, he later lettered in cross-country running on the high school's varsity squad. His stamina was remarkable considering a portion of one lung had been removed due to infection. In addition, doctors found it necessary to remove several ribs following an extended bout with osteomyelitis.

After receiving two college degrees and a number of academic honors, Smitty went on to become a career employee with the National Park Service. He and his wife, Shawn, are avid hikers and explorers wherever life takes them. Over the past several years, they have hiked the entire Pacific Crest Trail. They continue with similar challenges throughout the Americas as well as many distant lands.

Occasional surgeries during the past few decades are only bumps in the road for Smitty. He continues to exemplify the courage and determination that enabled him to recover from the Otokomi bear attack. Smitty's thoughts regarding his life's journey since the grizzly mauling provide a remarkable insight into the qualities of a true survivor.

In retrospect...

Yes, this day forever changed my life. However, if you were to ask me, "If you could do it over again, would you avoid the bear encounter?" To this, I would say, "No." The experience, however horrifying and painful, led me to where I am now...to find my soul mate, Shawn. It led me to see life from a far different perspective and to discern textures of life I may not have noticed otherwise.

I guess the worst day of my life paved the way for the best days of my life to come. It seems, now, as if that were the plan all along. Why, otherwise, would

Smitty Parratt (left) returns to Otokomi Lake with ranger naturalist Charles Scribner (right).

we have had premonitions of the attack before it happened? Questions, questions and where are the answers? What happens when you die? Why didn't I die?

What is the meaning behind it all? Forty-seven years later and counting, I still ponder these questions, questions that have yet to yield answers, only intuitions. Perhaps, they hold a sense of the way it might have been and, yet still may be.

17

THE ROGUE GRIZZLY

July 1961 – Many Glacier

"I'm afraid this grizzly is going to be trouble for us. You're all aware that he's been hanging out in the area for two weeks now. Worse yet, he just doesn't seem to have the slightest fear of humans." Larry Dale, Many Glacier Area Ranger, was briefing his park service employees at our weekly Monday morning meeting. He warned us to watch for the large, marauding male bear who had most likely wandered in from the remote Cracker Lake area. Over the past few days, the rogue bruin had raided several unattended campsites in the adjacent Swiftcurrent Campground and had chased a frightened family into their trailer.

More importantly, a day earlier, the bear had bluff-charged a couple nearby, further demonstrating a fearless attitude toward people. In this instance the bluff or identity charge included posturing wherein the grizzly bounded aggressively toward the pair. With arched back, the bruin slowly approached, slamming his feet against the ground and growling continually. Fortunately, the bear broke off this theatrical display and then stopped abruptly about thirty feet from the couple. Then, with typical grizzly unpredictability, he turned and left without further incident. The terrified pair fortunately stood their ground. Running would have most certainly triggered the bruin's predatory instincts. It can be stated that, in a foot race with a grizzly, humans seldom win. Such a confrontation has often ended with tragic results.

Many Glacier had long been a favorite haunt for grizzly bears. Most grizzlies wandered the upper slopes which led to the peaks of the area and, fortunately, seldom came into contact with humans. This bruin seemed to be the exception. As he developed a taste for humans' leftovers, he'd begun to associate the scent of people with food...a potentially deadly combination for both bear and human. Each day, the grizzly would appear on the outskirts of the campground or at the Swiftcurrent store and cabins nearby. The beast had been seen rummaging through garbage cans or scavenging for food scraps in campsites.

I was enjoying my second summer as a fireguard at Many Glacier Ranger Station. Over the past two summers, my boss, Larry, and I worked closely on various projects around the station and nearby fire cache. The entire complex used a road loop which ran behind the ranger station and then through the area that housed park service employees in cabins and trailers. At Larry Dale's request, two bear traps had been brought over from Saint Mary Ranger Station in an attempt to capture the grizzly alive. One was set up near the campground and the other within the park service complex nearby. Each trap consisted of a large culvert-style enclosure mounted on two axles which could be towed like a trailer. One end was held open by a latch that allowed the bear to enter. The opposite end was enclosed by a fixed set of bars and a bait hanger where an opened can of salmon was attached. When the bear entered the trap and pulled at the bait, the gate behind the animal was released, slamming down to take the bear captive.

A week passed as patrol rangers and other park workers kept surveillance on the bear's movements throughout the day and much of the night. Lured by the scent of the bait, this particular grizzly approached the traps numerous times but warily refused to enter. The traps remained empty. Word of the troublesome Many Glacier grizzly traveled quickly and often surfaced as one of the main topics of discussion throughout the park. As a consequence, all tent campers were asked to leave the area, haunted by the knowledge of the bear's presence. Appropriately, very few visitors were seen hiking any of the nearby trails. It seemed the large grizzly had, indeed, taken control of Many Glacier, growing bolder as each day passed. The ever-popular trail to Iceberg Lake was closed after the big bear was spotted near that trailhead. Nearby Redrock Lake trail was shut down the following day.

It became apparent to park officials that this brazen grizzly had no intention of leaving the Many Glacier area. He had found an easy food source and was now hooked on garbage. To the bear's keen sense of smell, the scent of humans meant food was sure to be nearby. At this point, the bear was said to be human-conditioned. Realizing serious human injury or death was inevitable if the situation continued, park officials reluctantly gave the order to shoot the bear. Even during this early period of the 1960's, destroying a large, majestic animal such as a grizzly was not taken lightly in a national park setting.

The morning the order reached his desk, Larry and I set out to end the bear's marauding spree. Initially, we parked his pickup within sight of the park service residential area. Ideally, the plan was to put the big bear down within the administrative complex out of view of the park's visitors. Such an event was certain to be unsettling to bystanders. On this particular morning, the bear had been sighted making his customary circuit, prompting us to be on alert. Our radio buzzed as a heads up came in from the patrol ranger. "He's coming your way Larry...just chased a guy into his camper."

With grim resolve, Larry responded, "Uh, ten-four Jim, he should be showing up any time now." Suddenly, emerging from behind the ranger station, the big bear spied our pale green park service truck. Immediately, he spun around and sprinted into a grove of trees near Swiftcurrent Creek.

Larry gave his .30-06 rifle a final check. I readied a second rifle as a backup. We sat there waiting in the safety of the truck as the minutes ticked by. Finally, Larry remarked dryly, "This grizzly is a smart one...he recognizes park service vehicles and he's avoiding them." Then with a look of determination, Larry picked up the radio and announced his decision to continue the pursuit using his family station wagon as a decoy for the wary grizzly. Next, he asked the patrol ranger to drive his cruiser through all inhabited areas broadcasting a request through his loudspeaker for everyone to remain inside. As we put our plan into action, the bear had again begun rummaging through the campground.

We quickly made the switch, climbing into Larry's station wagon. I felt the tension ratchet up measurably. Larry quickly drove behind the fire cache and pulled off the road. He whispered, "If this guy follows his usual route, he should be into the trash here soon." He nodded toward the garbage cans that were a mere fifty feet away. "I want to bring him down with one clean shot. If one shot doesn't do it, you're my backup with the other rifle."

My thoughts drifted to evenings of early season target practice with Larry at the Lake Sherburne dam. Located just outside the park on the Blackfeet Indian Reservation, the dam had been a safe location where we could spend time honing our skills with the government-issue rifles. We had to be prepared. But, paper targets were one thing, and a fearless live grizzly, quite another.

I can remember sitting there watching as Larry fidgeted nervously with the steering wheel. I noted his somber expression which mirrored the serious nature of the task which awaited us. His anxiety was contagious. I sensed a sudden, keen adrenaline rush as we both realized the final confrontation would be upon us very soon. I glanced over at Larry. His face was grim with concentration. Lives were at stake here, ours at the very least.

We both spotted the familiar cinnamon-colored bear at the same time. The large, dish-shaped face and the hump atop the massive shoulders made it clear that this was the grizzly. A hoarse whisper broke the silence, "Mark, no noise now. This is it." As we slid quietly out of the vehicle and stood motionless, the great bear stopped and turned to face us. In one swift motion, Larry carefully lifted his rifle, took aim and fired. The massive grizzly went down. Then, just as quickly, he regained his footing and charged straight at us. Time stood still. Suddenly, the entire scene seemed surreal. As the bear closed the distance between us, Larry quickly fired a second shot. The impact knocked the bear down once again. But then, just as before, he staggered to his feet and came for us. Larry yelled, "Shoot, Mark!" With the rifle butt pulled tightly against my shoulder, I rapidly fired two shots as the bear closed the distance between us. As the bullets found their mark, the grizzly dropped to the ground just ten feet from where we stood. With the bear still moving about as he struggled to regain his footing, Larry yelled, "Shoot! I'm jammed." I don't remember his final frantic words, but I felt the rifle butt pound my shoulder as I fired once more toward the bear's neck. The great beast, at last, slumped to the ground and lay still. In the wake of the violence, the silence that followed seemed overwhelming.

Finally, a ragged sigh burst from my lips. I realized my heart was pounding wildly. My legs trembled visibly and, for a moment, I wondered if they would continue to hold me upright. After several seconds, content the saga was finished, we dropped our rifles onto the car seat and sank to the ground. It was deathly quiet as we fixed our gaze on the huge hulk of the bruin as he lay motionless only a few feet from us. My throat was dry as I discovered I was temporarily speechless. I noted, with some surprise, that my hands were shaking uncontrollably. After a few moments spent regaining our composure, Larry turned to face me, a smile of respect replacing his look of concern. He found his voice and then, with his customary authority, reached out a hand to help me up, saying, "Come on buddy…we've got ourselves a bear to move out." Then, in softer tones, he added, "Glad we had that extra firepower…my rifle jammed. First time it's ever done that."

My rifle actually had been a part of bringing the big grizzly down. I felt joy in helping to bring the bear's reign of terror to an end. However, I also felt a certain sadness that this beautiful animal no longer breathed and roamed the land of its birth. I had neither shot nor killed anything before this day. In retrospect, I must say it was an experience I have never forgotten nor completely reconciled in my conscience.

The sharp crack of the rifles and the commotion that followed had brought out a number of fellow rangers as well as their families. A quiet circle of humanity gathered there, surrounding the body of the big bear. Within view of the curious onlookers, Larry and a fellow ranger examined the dead bruin carefully and determined that one slug had entered its chest and a second, the hind leg. Two more bullets had struck the bear's head with the fifth shot an apparent miss. In the final analysis, no one could say with certainty who had hit the grizzly or which volley had taken the great bear down. It took six men to load the massive animal into the back of a pickup truck that would transport the body to Saint Mary for examination by a park biologist a few hours later. The fearful saga drew to a close.

Word of the bear's demise traveled quickly and the following day, the Swiftcurrent Campground and cabin complex were, once again, buzzing with activity. Only a few random sightings of grizzly bears were made on distant trails the remainder of that summer in Many Glacier, but the renegade from Cracker Lake, who had commandeered our area and our lives for a time, would long live in our memories.

18
FATE IS A MOUNTAIN

June 1962 – Mount Henkel

The missing climbers were inexperienced and now long overdue. Raindrops and fierce winds began buffeting the windows of the ranger station as darkness set in. The Many Glacier-Saint Mary search and rescue team milled about the crowded room and, as a young fireguard of nineteen, I felt pride in being part of this close-knit and experienced crew. The mood grew somber as we realized that something had gone very wrong on that day in late June, 1962.

As the first light of day cast a faint pink glow on Many Glacier's rugged peaks, two young climbers began their ascent of Mount Henkel. Douglas Krouger, eighteen, and Jim Moylan, seventeen, were good friends and coworkers at the nearby Swiftcurrent general store. Indiana natives, they had come to the park seeking summer work and a chance to hike and climb in Glacier's alpine setting. A successful and exhilarating climb of nearby Altyn Peak a week earlier had buoyed their youthful confidence.

Now, the cool, crisp morning air spiked a sense of anticipation in the young men as they hiked the grassy slopes leading to the base of the towering peak. Following an established climbing route, their path bordered the edge of a large, tumbling stream off the south face of their objective. Excitement flooded their senses. Steeply rising cliffs would be the first real challenge of their day's climb.

We quickly focused, as Sub-District Ranger Robert Frauson broke the silence. "Listen up. We're going to head up to the base of the first set of cliffs and look for any sign of the climbers. If it gets too hairy up there, we'll pull back and try again at first light. Regardless of what happens tonight, it will be up to us to bring the climbers off the mountain one way or another. Everyone, check your climbing equipment and cold weather gear. This one could get rough."

Frauson had spent a number of weeks honing our climbing and rescue skills. A professional mountain climber and career park service ranger from Rocky Mountain National Park, the tall Norwegian had earned our unconditional respect. Previous rescues had taken place during daylight hours, but now, under cover of darkness and with no trail to guide us, our mission was sure to be a defining challenge. Nervous excitement rippled through the group.

Our rescue packs were crude and bulky by modern standards. Typical gear included our personal items, wool army blanket, sleeping bag, waterproof tarp, first aid equipment, aluminum hard hat, army surplus canteen, flashlight, crampons, ice axe, climbing rope, miscellaneous climbing hardware and military food rations. We took turns carrying the Stokes rescue litter and a heavy battery-operated military radio. Each fifty-pound pack provided human necessities for seventy-two hours. It would be men versus the mountain and its weather in a search for the missing.

The carbide lamps from our hardhats danced across the low forest cover as our team filed past the ranger station and headed upward. It was now 10:00 P.M. The trail led past a knot of the climbers' coworkers huddled near the general store. One young woman cried out, "Please bring them back alive. Oh, God. Please, please."

At 8,770 feet, Mount Henkel is considered a moderate climb, averaging seven hours round trip. The 4,000-foot ascent to the top of the last knife-edged pinnacle is known to be an exhilarating experience.

The rock faces, cliffs and chimneys of Glacier's towering peaks are mainly composed of structurally unsound shale, known by climbers as rotten rock. Additionally, many surfaces are littered with small broken pieces of rock called scree, making each step hazardous under the best of conditions.

Flashlights bobbed ahead as we spread out and scoured the lower grassy slopes for signs of the men. Suddenly, we heard a muffled shout from a team member poised at the edge of a large cascading stream. Instantly, many individual lights converged into one. Several fresh boot prints in the thin, muddy silt were proof that the climbers had plotted their course just west of the main stream bed. This preferred climbing route, marked by faint goat trails and small cairns, leads up into the great red shale basin, then continues toward the summit.

The wind pounded my rain parka as our group convened at the base of a large snowbank that covered the main streambed. After carefully searching the area and finding more boot prints in the snow, we moved to the base of the first rock face. Above lay the ghostly outlines of dark, misty cliffs and the unknown fate of two fragile human souls.

The radio crackled to life as team leader Robert Frauson discussed our options with park officials back at the ranger station.

Suddenly, a tremendous crash echoed from above. Instinctively, we all dove into crouching positions next to a nearby cliff face. A shower of loose scree was rapidly followed by the thunder of large boulders that careened over our heads and plummeted toward the valley below. Smaller pieces of snow and rock pelted our hard hats for several moments.

Shaken, we waited to make certain the rock slide had subsided. Frauson shouted, "This is far too dangerous. We have no choice but to pull off the mountain and hit it again at first light."

Glancing up into the darkness, he muttered, "Don't you just wonder what set that damn thing off?" With a collective sigh of relief, we quickly withdrew and headed back down the grassy slopes. It was 2:30 A.M. when we finally reached the Many Glacier Ranger Station.

Cold and weary, we collapsed on our cots for a brief hour's rest. With the excitement of the evening just past, sleep was all but impossible. From a nearby cot, someone asked, "Don't you wonder if those guys are alive? Do you suppose they saw our flashlights or heard our shouts?" Silence intervened as we pondered the questions. One thing for certain, the longer the climbers were out there, the more urgent our mission became.

A gentle mist sent rivulets down the window pane as a subdued group gathered just after 3:30 A.M. A hint of dawn could be seen on the eastern horizon. Ominous clouds encased Mt. Henkel's upper reaches, threatening to further complicate our efforts.

Beginning at a brisk pace, we skirted a series of small cliffs. Then, wet, low-growing grasses and unstable patches of shale temporarily slowed our progress. However, in an hour's time, we arrived at the site of the previous evening's rock slide. Looking about, we were amazed. The area where we had stood was now littered with enormous boulders. Indeed, we had been fortunate to escape injury or death the previous evening.

In the general store parking lot, far below us, an anxious crowd had gathered to watch the ongoing search. Peering through binoculars, they watched tiny figures rope themselves together, then follow a lead climber. As time passed, the spectators found their vision obscured by a thick cloud cover which gradually slipped down the mountain.

We made our way upward, pelted by light rain and then, snow. The dense fog quickly turned a difficult operation into a climber's nightmare. Visibility was reduced to less than ten feet as we struggled to make out the ghostly figures of our team members. Footing became precarious on the slippery rocks. The climbing ropes that tethered us together became our only safety net.

As the snowfall grew more intense, Frauson suddenly stopped and drew us into a huddle. His voice was hoarse in the wail of the driving wind. "This is it, guys. We'll search another five hundred feet up the climbing route. If they're not in that section of cliffs, we'll call it quits. It's just getting too dangerous up here. Remember our training. Work together and be safe. Let's go."

We struggled forward now, shouting the names of the missing. The faint echoes of our voices were muted by the winds. Progress slowed to a crawl as the freezing temperatures numbed our bodies and slowed our minds.

I had hiked and climbed in Glacier for fourteen summers of my young life. Now, for the first time in my memory, the invincible and immortal feeling of youth was missing. I was frightened. Really frightened. The looks on the faces of my partners mirrored my own unspoken fears.

Then, through the thin, cold air, Frauson's command jolted us to a stop. As we huddled on a narrow ledge, he told us that we had done our best and that to turn back was now a matter of our personal safety. With feelings of both regret and relief, we quickly prepared for our descent.

Suddenly, the howling wind eased and, in the silence that followed, a muted cry came from the fog-shrouded cliffs above. Ears straining, all heads jerked in the direction of the sound.

Two scouts painstakingly scaled the cliff and there, in the shelter of a large boulder, lay Douglas Krouger. The pale young man was obviously in shock and seriously injured. Surely, this discovery was a miracle. Had the strong winds continued, we would have begun our descent without hearing his cries for help. The climber most likely would have died from hypothermia within hours.

Groggy and weak, Krouger managed to point to our left and mutter, "Find Jim. Find Jim."

As first aid was administered, Frauson directed three of us to

The Rescue Crew.

Mount Henkel, left above Many Glacier

continue our search for Jim Moylan. Moments later, we discovered his lifeless body sprawled over a pile of broken rock not far away. Nausea gripped my stomach as the intensity of the moment sent shivers through me.

I recoiled. This was not how a climbing adventure in a beautiful alpine setting was supposed to end. I fought back tears as we wrapped the crumpled body in wool blankets and secured it on a ledge nearby. The location was marked with bright orange streamers tied to hastily constructed rock cairns.

A second recovery team would now be needed to bring Moylan's remains off the mountain. Our entire team would be needed to move the surviving climber to safety.

Krouger's preliminary diagnosis included head lacerations, possible internal bleeding and severe fractures of the right leg and shoulder.

Carefully loaded onto a blanket-covered Stokes litter, the young man was strapped in place and prepared for the descent. He appeared stable and was conscious for the duration of his arduous trip down the mountain. We roped up into two teams as Frauson directed the descent.

As if in mute celebration, sunlight suddenly poured down upon the mountain, warming us and buoying our spirits. The last vestiges of the storm passed on to the east.

It was 3:00 P.M. as our crew covered the remaining distance to the valley below. Enroute, we met the team who would retrieve the body of Jim Moylan. As we arrived at the Swiftcurrent parking lot, we were greeted by cheers and applause from the campers and coworkers gathered there. The celebration was short lived, however, as the group was informed of Moylan's death. Nearby, an ambulance stood waiting. A short time later, it sped away bearing Krouger to a Kalispell hospital.

Keenly aware of the ongoing rescue operations, several rangers' wives had prepared a pot luck dinner for our return. The meal was hot and there was plenty of it. As we ate, Frauson commended us for our effort. We had saved a human life and completed the operation without mishap.

Later that evening, while enjoying a hot shower, the events of the past two days swept over me. Tears of both joy and sadness tumbled down my cheeks in a sudden release of pent up emotion. The mountain had spared one life and taken another.

Several days later, Krouger summarized the fateful climb from his hospital bed. He spoke of an experience that began positively with the pair reaching Henkel's summit around noon the first day. The two had eaten lunch and admired the stunning panorama which surrounded them.

However, concern began to overtake the young men as the sky above them darkened. A rapidly developing storm system moved toward the summit where they stood. As gusty winds buffeted the area, they began a hurried descent by retracing their established climbing route. Upon reaching a point halfway down the mountain face, a driving rain and a dense layer of swirling clouds enveloped the young climbers.

With visibility reduced to only a few feet, they were compelled to make a decision; hunker down and wait for better visibility or go for it and continue their descent. Unaware of the duration or severity of the storm, the pair reasoned their best option was to seek a lower elevation. Once below the cloud ceiling, they felt they could reach the safety of the Many Glacier valley.

Believing they were on course, the men slowly moved down through the broken cliffs. With visibility rapidly deteriorating, Moylan took the lead. Within minutes, the pair unknowingly strayed off the main climbing route, finding themselves in a difficult section of steep pitches. As Krouger followed a few feet behind Moylan, he looked up to see his friend stumble, then disappear into the dense fog.

In panic, he peered into the abyss to see the faint outline of his companion far below. He detected slight movement, heard a groan, and then, silence. Anguished, he moved blindly through the fog and began climbing down a seam in the rock toward his fallen comrade. Then, in an instant, he lost his footing. Krouger faintly remembered tumbling downward, then darkness.

Later, as the young man awakened, a cool mist bathed his face. He was disoriented and gasping for breath, intense pain searing his body. Unable to sit up, he managed to turn over and slowly crawl to a large boulder, where he curled into a fetal position. Distraught and seriously injured, the young climber now found himself a prisoner of the mountain. His only companions now were the wail of the wind and the sounds of the rain.

Throughout the entire ordeal, Krouger confided he had never lost hope and believed all along that rescuers would find him alive. He managed to ward off hypothermia with the aid of a wool hat and a heavy parka, which he had donned for his descent. From where he lay on the cliff, he had not seen our lights nor heard our calls the previous evening.

Douglas Krouger was airlifted home after several weeks of hospitalization. Months later, he had largely recovered from his physical injuries. The recovery from his emotional scars was likely to take a lifetime.

Helicopters were not employed for search and rescue operations at the time of this story. Since then, they have played an increasingly active role. Climbing apparel, rescue equipment and communications have rapidly evolved since the Mount Henkel saga. The old vacuum tube portable radios of the 1960's were bulky, extremely heavy, and often unreliable. The hand-held digital radios and GPS units in use today exemplify the advances in technology which have occurred since that time. The aspects of climbing that remain constant, however, are the preparedness of the climber, the difficulty of the climb, ever-changing weather conditions…and, often, the hand of fate.

19

PIKE EYES

Monty knew, with certainty, that there were large great northern pike in Glacier's Lake Sherburne. Earlier that summer, he'd met up with a pair of Canadian fishermen who spoke of fishing the lake regularly over the years with considerable success. They told tales of great northern pike or northerns so large that landing them from shore was virtually impossible. With no access point or ramp from which to launch a boat, fishing from shore was an angler's only option.

Always up for a challenge, Monty ventured to the shores of the lake one morning in late July. As he set out down the trail, my young brother had no idea of the terror which lay beneath the murky waters of the lake that day. This would be one fishing adventure he would long remember.

By anyone's estimation, he was an outstanding fisherman. Monty possessed a special finesse, a know-how that made fishing truly an art form. He was known throughout the park as the young man who could catch fish practically anywhere, anytime.

As the sun warmed the morning air, with his fishing gear strapped to his backpack, Monty made his way around the northern end of Lake Sherburne on a portion of the Cracker Lake trail. Eventually, he left the pathway and hiked across the grassy meadows of Sherburne's south shore to a series of shallow fingers or lagoons. The beach there was covered with water-worn rocks mingled with open spots of soft clay silt. From the edge of Boulder Ridge's forested flanks, the shoreline dropped steeply down to the sandy coves.

This was prime grizzly bear country. There had been several

sightings of a good sized male grizzly roaming the lake's edge during the past few weeks. Monty had duly noted several of the bear's tracks on the trail earlier that morning. Now, he saw those same telltale imprints pressed deeply into the silt, mingling with those of his own boots. Wary, he continually glanced at the dense forest behind him and scanned the beaches on both sides of the lake. Not a living creature was in sight. Still, with grizzlies randomly patrolling the shoreline, a certain air of uneasiness persisted. He shuddered inwardly as he thought about the horrific   grizzly bear incident two summers earlier that nearly took the life of his younger brother, Smitty.

A week earlier, Monty had purchased a pair of six inch, red Daredevle lures. The Canadian fishermen felt that big lures sometimes caught big fish. That made perfect sense to Monty as he snapped one of the large spoons onto his steel leader. His spinning reel was spooled with fifteen pound test line, enough, he felt, to play out almost any large pike.

Making a quick visual check for bears once again, he cautiously approached a nearby lagoon and felt a heady anticipation rise in his chest. He began making long casts into the main body of the lake, reeling the big spoon slowly through the shallow waters. The lure made a whistling sound each time it was flung across the surface of the lake. Water plants were thick at the bottom of the silted backwaters, a perfect hiding place for resting pike. Within minutes, Monty caught and released two small northerns. Patiently moving along the edge of the lagoon, he continued his spin casting.

Suddenly, a strong tug announced the presence of a larger pike. A quick upward jerk of the pole's tip set the hook. Before long he realized he'd caught the attention of a good-sized fish, a real fighter. After wrestling the taut line for some ten minutes, the fish finally tired of the struggle and sidled up toward the beach. Wearing a leather glove on his right hand, Monty carefully pulled the long reptilian looking creature out of the water. Grabbing the back of the pike's large head with his gloved hand, he surveyed the remarkable predator. Suddenly, with a powerful twist, the large jaws clamped down on his glove. Fortunately, the needle sharp teeth just grazed the edge of the leather covering his thumb. Monty quickly struck the fish on the head with a piece of driftwood, ending the struggle. This one was a keeper. The large northern measured thirty one inches in length and weighed in at ten pounds.

After resting a bit, Monty dressed out his catch, wrapped it in a special piece of canvas and stuffed it into his rucksack. Bear wary, he realized the scent of fresh fish wafting through the air could surely attract any grizzly that happened to be nearby. He was careful to throw the entrails and head of the fish far out into the lake and made certain to clean the fishy odor from his hands. Content with his success, he sensed it was time to head back.

Shouldering his pack, he began his trek, skirting the forest that grew just above the water. As he glanced at the remaining lagoons near the end of the lake, a peculiar sight caught his eye. In a deep finger, he spotted a half dozen large objects hovering just below the surface of the water. He dropped down the steep incline and carefully approached the lagoon. He caught his breath as he noted movement in the water. Closer examination revealed he had come upon a school of very large northern pike. He slowly crept closer and gasped at what he saw. Two of the fish had to be at least four feet in length, possibly even longer.

Monty found his excitement difficult to contain. These fish were unlike anything he'd seen before in Glacier's waters. Using a low embankment nearby as cover, he quickly prepared his spinning outfit. Nervously, he whipped the top of his pole and flung the Daredevle far into the slender finger of water. As the lure splashed near the resting giants, he held his breath. There was no response.

Reeling in, he again tossed his line toward the opening of the inlet. By occasionally jerking the tip of his pole, the spoon presented an erratic motion. At once, the largest of the basking northerns rose and hit the spinning lure hard. As the pole bent double, the mammoth fish twisted and turned in an attempt to throw off the treble hook that had snared him. Monty briefly spied the white underbelly of the northern, rolling just beneath the murky waters.

He felt his breath catch in his throat, stunned by the immensity of the creature.

After several more rolls, the giant turned and left the shallow, sheltered waters of the lagoon, heading out toward the main body of the lake. With the drag on his reel set as tightly as he dared, Monty hung on, his throbbing pole still bent double. The great pike slowly, deliberately continued to swim toward the middle of the lake. Now sweating profusely, Monty had already given up any hope of turning the great fish around. Against the rapid, clicking sounds of the drag, he watched as 250 yards of monofilament line rapidly disappeared into the depths. Now at last, he could see the spool's chrome center. What first had seemed like a generous supply of fishing line suddenly didn't seem like much at all.

And then, with only a few feet of line left on the reel, the fish abruptly turned and began to slowly head back toward the lagoon. Quickly reeling to keep the line taut, Monty kept pace with the incoming monster. Wet line began to accumulate on the spool as the pike continued its peculiar course straight toward him.

Thoughts ricocheted through his mind. "Never had a fish act like this before. Maybe, just maybe, I can land this thing."

As the big pike approached, Monty took a wide stance on the steep bank in preparation for what might happen next. Digging the heels of his logger's boots into the rocky silt, he kept a steady eye on the water.

Amazingly, now only ten feet away, the northern continued swimming directly toward him. As its size and length became apparent, Monty began to tremble. Standing there alone on the shores of the great lake, he realized he'd more than met his match. Taking a quick estimate, he told himself the fish had to be close to four feet in length, a good quarter of it taken up by its massive head.

Suddenly, two bulging eyes were fixed on Monty. When the huge fish broke the water, a red spoon could be seen dangling from the corner of its mouth. As my brother held tightly to the pole, his boots suddenly lost traction on the steep bank. He found himself abruptly propelled downward on his back. Reaching the edge of the water with a splash, Monty struggled to regain his stance. An unnerving panic gripped him as he tried to distance himself from the pike's steady glare.

Then, without warning, the huge fish lunged from the water, its great mouth agape. The jagged teeth rimming its powerful jaws grabbed Monty's right boot at the ankle. The pressure was amazing. A harsh jolt of terror seared though him as he struggled to free himself.

Momentarily recalling tactics he'd used in his days of high school wrestling, Monty dropped his pole and braced himself against the bank. The body of the great northern, its wide mouth temporarily imprisoning his leg, made a quick barrel roll. In disbelief, Monty felt himself being flipped onto his stomach. Time seemed to stand still.

With one final lunge, the giant released its grip. His mind racing, Monty quickly grabbed his pole by its midsection and hung on. Giving a parting lash with its tail, the northern turned and once again headed for open water. Hands shaking, Monty shifted his grip on the pole, grasping the handle as tightly as he could. As the rapid click of the drag continued, the line tilted steeply downward as the predator dove.

Still shaken, he watched the line quickly disappearing from his reel until it abruptly came to the end of the spool. The pole bent double as he struggled to maintain his grip. Then, with a loud ping, the broken line slackened on the water's surface. The fish was gone. Glancing briefly at the bare reel, he quickly scrambled up the rise to higher ground. An examination of his boot revealed three broken, razor sharp teeth embedded in the black leather. He stood there trembling, intensely aware of the pounding of his heart.

Suddenly, he felt an eagerness to distance himself from the troubling event. Hefting his pack, he quickly headed down the beach and then made his way up the trail. Slowed by his sore ankle, he continued onward as fast as his legs would allow.

Upon reaching the dirt track, Monty stopped to check out the source of his pain. As he began to untie his boot, he detected a slight movement behind him. Quickly turning, he squinted against

A muddy Lake Sherburne in the Spring.

the glare of the sun. There, along the shoreline, his eyes caught the form of a grizzly. The beast pawed the very spot where Pike Eyes had attacked only moments earlier. He quickly retied his boot, wishing only to get well beyond the bruin's field of vision. Ignoring his throbbing ankle, once again, he set off down the trail. Quickening his pace, Monty glanced over his shoulder now and then. The bear quickly became a tiny dot roaming the distant beach. Weary and worn by the experience, he finally walked into the hotel parking lot close to an hour later. After dropping his gear into the trunk of the car, he quickly pulled off his boots. His right ankle was red and swollen. To his relief, the skin didn't appear to be broken. The high top leather boots had saved him from more serious injury. Using his fishing pliers, Monty carefully pulled the jagged fragments out of his boot. Each broad, triangular tooth was a good half inch wide. Once again, the thought of the northern's gnashing jaws caused him to shudder.

Nearby, a park ranger could be seen posting a hand written notice at the trailhead to Cracker Lake. It read, "Warning: Grizzly Bear Activity on this Trail." Monty approached the ranger and, after reading the sign, relayed his recent sighting of the big bear. The

Pike for Dinner.

ranger thanked him for the update and then asked, "So, how was the fishing?"

Monty shrugged his shoulders and replied, "It was good, but I don't know that I'd try it again this summer." True to his word, he did not return to Lake Sherburne that season or for several to follow. Three years later, he chose to fish the lake, bringing along several colleagues with whom he worked on the park service blister rust crew. They all caught northerns that day and, fortunately, saw no sign of bear. As a companion passed comment over lunch about what a peaceful fishing spot they'd chosen, Monty smiled that memorable smile and then began to relate the tale of Pike Eyes.

20

THE OLD
BLISTER RUST DAYS

Summer 1963 - Monty Parratt – Dry Fork Valley

High school had just ended for me in early June of 1963. I skipped graduation ceremonies and caught a plane for Great Falls, Montana. I climbed on board, eager to see Glacier again and anticipating the best summer of my life. My plane set down in Montana, at last, and my brother Mark was there to meet me. We threw my gear in the back seat and he drove us northwest along the Rocky Mountain Front to Glacier National Park. After a short, satisfying visit with my brother, he dropped me off at the tent camp

Before joining the blister rust crew in 1963, Monty found work as an attendant at Smiley's Gas Station in East Glacier.

in West Glacier, just inside the park boundary.

I had been hired as a laborer on the blister rust crew for the park service. I showed up along with forty other eighteen to twenty-year old college students from across the country. Much like a military boot camp, we were assigned tents and cots. In fact, we soon learned that our camp bosses were ex-Navy officers. They put the fear of God in us. We did the best we could to keep them happy by promptly doing exactly what they asked. If we did foul up, we'd end up back on the plane headed for home. A few vigorous weeks of training included physical conditioning and the specifics of blister rust.

Blister rust is a fungus which attacks western white and whitebark pines. In certain cool, humid conditions, wind carries the fungal spores from the genus *Ribes* (currants and gooseberries), an intermediate blister rust host, to the white pines nearby. The rust or fungus then enters the tree through the needles and works its way down to the base of the tree. Eventually, the disease girdles the tree, killing it.

The job of the blister rust crewman or blister ruster, was to carry a forty-five pound tank of anti-fungal chemical (phyto-actin) mixed in a fuel oil base. In a methodical manner, we sprayed as many white pines as possible. For blister rusters, saving the beautiful trees was akin to saving a piece of the earth. Carrying these tanks around all day was hard work, and it didn't take long for us to reach peak physical condition. As a result, we often ended up on crews fighting fires in Glacier. Back in those days, we always had work. Even on rainy days when we couldn't spray, we built trails, bridges, and did any other work our camp bosses ordered.

A few weeks into our training at West Glacier, our crew bosses asked for eight volunteers to work for the summer at Oldman Lake. Having hiked in this backcountry area a few years earlier, I knew that this was the place for me. I told my fellow crew member, Curt Buchholtz, how beautiful it would be to work out of Oldman Lake. I envisioned climbing, hiking, and fishing right out of our camp. Curt listened and promptly made up his mind to join the crew as well. As it turned out, we had a close-knit team who worked hard and played hard together.

We packed our gear and jumped in the truck headed for Two Medicine. Upon arriving there, Curt and I, along with our foreman, Bill Gardner, hiked up the Dry Fork trail that passes to the north of Rising Wolf Mountain. The trail meandered up into a narrow valley with mountains rising on all sides. We finally reached our camp at Oldman Lake by early afternoon.

After a quick snack, we began setting up tent cabins. These house-like tents had canvas walls stretched over wood frames with wood plank floors. We then set about other chores that prepared the camp for summer.

The next day, I was assigned the grueling task of digging out the latrine. The rocky soil made it a slow job. It took the entire day to dig a pit six feet deep and five feet wide. I took plenty of ribbing about this assignment, learning quickly that taking harassment was part of the training. We built a wood frame above the hole with the opening looking straight up at Rising Wolf Mountain. I remember watching many sunsets sitting on that very latrine over the summer months.

On one of these occasions, I spotted a grizzly bear climbing Rising Wolf. The marvelous creature ran continuously up sliding shale, traveling some 4,000 feet in only eight minutes to the mountain's summit. I learned quickly that if a griz wanted to catch me, it would.

Our camp was made up of three tents, one being a sleep tent for our crew. It was outfitted with bunks and a little pot-bellied stove for when it got cold. The tent across from our sleeping quarters was the cook tent. We were blessed with a wonderful cook, Miriam Wilson. The crew really liked him. He treated and fed us like royalty. A very cold spring-fed creek kept our food chilled. The third was our supply tent which held our tools and tanks for blister rust duties. A black barrel served as our shower.

On a typical day, we would wake up at 6:00 A.M. and head for the cook tent. For breakfast, we'd devour dozens of eggs and large quantities of bacon, pancakes, toast and cereal with milk and juice. Evenings, we would go to the cook tent and make our lunches for the next day. I would make four sandwiches, and then grab an apple and an orange for my flour sack lunch bag.

After breakfast, I'd tie the sack to my belt, throw on my hard hat, grab my forty-pound spray tank, and then pick up two fifty-pound jeep cans full of chemical. With one jeep can in each hand, I'd head up the steep trail which led out of camp to the main trail. We always carried the bulk of our chemical out in the morning.

Using heavy white string, we divided the ancient whitebark pine forest into lanes. Each of us was responsible for a section. When, at last, we came to a double string, we knew that was the end of our particular lane. We would then hike back to the trail and find another lane to spray.

We had to find every white pine in our assigned lane. The bosses would follow behind, bringing us back to start over, if they found that we had missed one. Needless to say, we became very vigilant about our work. We traveled over and under logs and through rough terrain, always carrying the heavy tanks on our backs.

Our only stop was a half-hour break when we would devour our lunch and drink a full canteen of water. My clothes were drenched with sweat most of the time. We had to be in our lanes by 8:00 A.M. and could not leave the work area until 4:30 P.M.

At the end of the day, we would hike back down to camp, fill our tanks, chop wood, and clean up before an incredible supper of mashed potatoes, breaded veal cutlets, vegetables and lots of thick gravy. We drank huge quantities of milk and kept our packer, Gene Brash, busy most of the week hauling chemical and food.

After dinner, I would run up the trail about three miles to the lake for some fishing. The huge cutthroat trout of Oldman Lake were very fussy and hard to catch. I would fish until the alpenglow disappeared, head back to camp, then sleep and dream.

Our days off were spent climbing and hiking. One day Curt and I climbed to the summit of 9,518-foot Rising Wolf Mountain. It took us a couple hours of one step forward, then two steps back to

Oldman Lake in the Dry Fork Valley.

get there. From the summit, the view was great and it was fun to look down upon our camp and the areas where we worked. Next, Curt and I moved along the knife-edged ridge above Boy Lake and Young Man Lake and onto the base of Flinsch Peak. We climbed the 9,225-foot peak for spectacular views of Buffalo Woman Lake, the Nyack Valley and towering Mount Stimson. The sharp tooth of Mt. St. Nicholas, the park's highest peak, reached for the blue sky above. Curt and I then headed over to our next objective, Mt. Morgan. From its summit, we could see down the Dry Fork Valley toward Lower Two Medicine Lake. From this point, we could also see Cut Bank and Pitamakan Passes and the lakes below.

With a full day of hiking and climbing behind us, we decided to head back to camp. Our decision was a good one because, in our exuberance, we didn't notice the thunderheads fast approaching. Thunder and lightning chased us down Pitamakan Pass. When we eventually reached our camp, it felt good to light up that old pot-bellied stove.

The next day we were prepared to carry the chemical back up the hill to our assigned work areas. On one occasion, I carried four tanks strapped to one another on my back and two jeep cans in each hand. I carried the four-hundred pounds of chemicals uphill for a mile. This established a record for carrying the heaviest load the longest distance without rest. Great contests sprang up among the workers, whether it be felling trees or chopping fire wood. These competitions really got us in shape. We were lean and mean and there were few tasks too tough for us.

My camp boss, Jerry Hassinger, gave me many rough assignments as I seemed to enjoy a little physical punishment. One day, he ordered me to spray the cirque of Young Man Lake. I had to leave camp with a tank and two jeep cans full of chemical. First, I hauled them across the large stream that flowed through the valley. I plowed my way through thick patches of snowbush. In some places, I had to forge, head first, and then twist sideways to get the jeep cans through the brush. When I fell, I had to slip my tank off, pick myself up and then put the tank back on and reassemble the jeep cans. It took an hour to bushwhack to the cliffs overlooking Young Man Lake and over another hour to make my way up, then down to the lakeshore. Once I reached the lake, I strung up my own lanes and began to spray the white pine.

One day at Young Man Lake, I saw a lynx for the first time. I felt privileged to view an animal that is seldom seen in the wilds. At day's end, I would have to hike out and bushwhack on my own time. I would generally get back to camp tired and very hungry.

I finished spraying around Young Man Lake in one week. After that lonely week on my own, it was good to be back working with fellow crewmembers. We spent the remainder of the summer spraying the valley in the Oldman Lake area.

Blister Rust ultimately got the best of most white pine trees in Glacier National Park. The old growth whitebark pine forest in the Oldman Lake area was one of the most majestic stands in the world. Despite the best efforts of National Park Service crews like Monty's and massive amounts of chemical application, most of the ancient whitebark pine in this valley and around the park stand dead, whitewashed snags, victims of a past invader.

21
LONE CLIMBER MISSING

July 1963 – Going-to-the-Sun Mountain

David Wilson, twenty-one, and his older brother, Steve, had signed on to work for a park service blister rust crew out of the Two Medicine area that fateful summer of 1963.

One crisp Sunday morning on the 26th of July, David set out alone, intent on scaling Glacier National Park's rugged Going-to-the-Sun Mountain. Later that day, one of Wilson's friends discovered a handwritten note indicating his intentions. At 9,540 feet above sea level, the imposing alpine peak dominates the northern skyline of the vast Saint Mary valley below.

The park's famous road over the Continental Divide, the Going-to-the-Sun Road, is aptly named for the towering mountain landmark. Wilson had chosen the popular, rugged west face climbing route. Technically, this approach commands a strenuous effort in order to master a series of moderate pitches followed by several more difficult Class IV sections near the summit. These segments require rock climbing experience and the utmost care to avoid a misstep. Brittle and unstable shale creates cliffs that often come apart in one's hands. The loose scree only compounds the danger of the climbing experience.

By late evening Monday, July 27th, chatter over the park's C.B. radio system indicated growing concern over a missing man. When Wilson failed to report for work the morning following his departure, his brother, Steve, and other coworkers alerted park service officials. It was later confirmed that Wilson had successfully hitchhiked to the drop-off point for his climb. Why hadn't he returned?

Our Many Glacier search and rescue team was a veteran group. Over the past four summers, the crew had completed over a dozen rescue operations throughout the park. The summer of 1963 also marked my fourth season as both a fireguard and as an active member of the team. It was an honor to be part of this elite and close knit group of vigorous young men.

Summoned to the ranger station on that summer evening, we listened intently as Area Ranger Larry Dale, spoke in hushed tones. "As you've already heard, we have a missing climber. David Wilson works for the park service. He is one of us. We know he attempted the climb and should have returned by early evening. Going-to-the-Sun can be one tough haul. I can't imagine why anyone would ever try to climb it alone. If he doesn't show up by seven, tomorrow morning, we'll begin a search."

A flood of emotions overtook me as we approached the fire cache to set our rescue packs in order. While checking my equipment, thoughts of both the imposing mountain and the missing climber consumed me. Going-to-the-Sun Mountain had not been kind to me in the past. During a recreational climb the previous summer, I'd slipped and fallen some fifty feet down one of its rocky slopes. With three broken ribs, I had gingerly retreated with the help of my climbing companion, Jim Stewart. The fall had left me with a renewed respect for the dangerous sport as well as for the daunting peak. The impending search effort would provide me with a return to Going-to-the-Sun and a chance to help another climber. Admittedly, it also offered the opportunity to regain a certain part of my self confidence that I'd forfeited the day of my own tumble.

The cool morning air sharpened our senses as we swiftly loaded rescue equipment into waiting pickup trucks. For an anxious group of young men, the forty-five minute drive to the staging area seemed endless. By 7:00 A.M., our team finally arrived at Siyeh Bend, a wide pull off along Going-to-the-Sun Road that would serve as our base of operations.

Hailed by fellow search and rescue crew members from Saint Mary Ranger Station, we joined other climbers milling about.

Suddenly edgy and eager to begin the search, a sense of growing anticipation seemed to overtake the group. Small talk amongst the men was muted by the crescendo of waterfalls tumbling from the cliffs nearby. Standing there, one could only marvel at the lofty reaches of Going-to-the-Sun Mountain. The massive alpine peak, object of our attention, steeply rose some 6,000 feet into the heavens above us. A light breeze carried the fragrance of lush vegetation fed by the many streams cascading down the mountain's flanks. Billowy white clouds provided sharp contrast with a deep azure blue sky, creating a dramatic backdrop.

At length, a familiar voice beckoned to us. Drawn together in a tight knot at the edge of the road, we listened as Saint Mary Sub-District Ranger Robert Frauson, began to speak. He was revered by all. Once a proud member of the army's elite mountain ski battalion during World War II, the towering, ruddy-faced Norwegian inspired abiding confidence. Spreading out a topographic map on the hood of a nearby truck, he outlined our search plan for the day. He noted that our efforts would be assisted by the park's fire spotter plane as well as a helicopter.

Final search instructions were given and we departed. Our orange climbing helmets formed a line which bobbed along the edge of the parking lot, disappearing, at last, in the direction of the steep trail. In bright sunshine, the Piegan Pass trail fork led the group across two large streams and through dense thickets of subalpine fir.

At a point known as the great avalanche area, we left the trail and scrambled, cross country, up the base of the great mountain. Eventually, the team spread out and began to carefully comb the slopes, finally reaching the base of the steep pitches which led to the summit. If Wilson had miscued and fallen, the rock chimneys and spires would certainly be logical places for a detailed search.

Adding to the intensity of the operation, the spotter plane, with an experienced climber aboard, scoped the entire mountain for several hours before nightfall. The aerial and ground searches that took place that day would, remarkably, yield nothing. A setting sun cast ever-deepening shadows as the group of weary young men retraced their steps to the base camp. A sense of frustration followed in each footstep. At the day's beginning, we'd all felt certain we would find Dave Wilson. Where was he? What would tomorrow bring?

On day two, we left Many Glacier before sunrise and headed out once again toward the staging area. Arriving to a bustle of activity, we received instructions for the day. A total of twenty men would search a wide swath of terrain that covered the entire west face of Going-to-the-Sun Mountain. Other climbers would scour the slopes of nearby Matahpi Peak and Mount Siyeh.

Another perfect day dawned with light winds and a cloudless sky. The men methodically worked their way along the steep trail and then, up the cliffs to the saddle which lay between Matahpi and Going-to-the-Sun. Crews painstakingly bisected the lower mountainside with hundreds of feet of white string that crossed the rugged terrain like a checkerboard. Searchers meticulously scanned each section, working slowly up the mountain's flanks. As the search was completed in one section, the string was moved upward into the next.

The spotter plane continued to circle overhead...banking, climbing, and then swooping down to search a particular area of interest. The drone of the single engine aircraft sent eerie echoes ricocheting off the towering peaks nearby. Providing a counterpoint was the fluttering sound of a brightly colored helicopter as it moved about the mountain like a large dragonfly. Sounds of the aircraft overhead muffled occasional shouts among the climbers.

A small group had searched the mountain's summit earlier but failed to find the climbing register, a key which could provide important evidence in solving this mystery. Intent on a second, more detailed examination of the area, ranger Willie Colony, chose four of us to accompany him. Colony was a respected alpine climber who had honed his search and rescue skills in the rugged Rocky Mountain National Park. Under his guidance, we carefully negotiated the steep chimneys, reaching our goal at last. Resting

Searchers examine possible signs of David Wilson's route on the west face of Going-to-the-Sun Mountain.

briefly at the summit, we marveled at the sight of peaks and spires which pierced the skyline for over fifty miles in any direction.

At the summit of each peak, climbers would traditionally erect a cairn, a tall pinnacle of carefully positioned rocks. Within the cairn would be stowed the climbers' register, a small notebook and pencil encased in a hefty section of galvanized pipe. As was the custom, climbers would sign the register, indicating the date of their ascent and often a few comments regarding their climb.

After probing through the rocky shale for an hour, we located the climber's register buried near the base of the cairn. To our amazement, Wilson's signature was there. He had successfully reached the summit of Going-to-the-Sun Mountain on Sunday. What an eerie feeling it was to view the name of the missing man. He had stood in this very spot. Where could he be? Where could our efforts to find him have failed? It was as if David Wilson had literally vanished into the thin alpine air.

We quickly radioed the news of our find to base camp. Over the radio, a voice responded, "Ah, ten-four. Good work, guys." There was a pause, and then, "Wow, this is getting spooky. What are we missing here?" Day two of the search ended several hours later in the splendor of a beautiful Montana sunset. Once again, darkness fell on the great mountain.

The massive search effort had now spanned two days and was beginning to attract regional and national media attention. During daylight hours, large numbers of curious onlookers jammed the Siyeh Bend base camp. Staring upward, countless eyes scanned the mountainsides, following the movements of the climbers.

The possibility of finding David Wilson alive was diminishing with each passing day. Temperatures above the 7,500-foot level were sinking well below freezing during the hours of darkness. If the man were still alive, hypothermia and dehydration would certainly have begun to take their toll.

Thursday dawned and the third day of the search began. By now, the exhaustive effort involved more than thirty experienced climbers.

Cold winds, which gusted down the slopes over the Continental Divide, spit dust and gravel at the men. The helicopter from West Glacier was grounded for most of the day due to the gales.

Larry Dale and I were climbing up a steep ravine when I heard a familiar voice. I swung around to see my brother, Monty. He had joined the effort, along with his blister rust crew, in the search for their missing colleague. We hugged and chatted briefly.

The surprise meeting on this cold afternoon reminded us of the wonderful times we had known climbing and hiking during our younger years. Hugging once more, we parted. Seeing my brother was a wonderful surprise, infusing me with warmth and renewed energy.

A short time later, we met up with Steve Wilson, brother of the missing man. How strange to see my own brother and then, within the span of five minutes, the brother of the lost climber. Suddenly,

The east face of Going-to-the-Sun Mountain drops precipitously into the Saint Mary Valley. Sun Point junction and parking lot are visible below.

the tone of the search had taken on new meaning for me: Monty, robust and alive and the missing climber's brother, grieving and in emotional pain. Love had instilled in Steve Wilson the remarkable courage necessary to climb the forbidding mountain in hopes of finding his only brother.

Upon our return to the camp, we caught a glimpse of Steve and his father, Paul, in a tearful embrace. Witnessing the poignant scene, Monty and I flung an arm around one another and then wordlessly parted.

Where was David Wilson and what had become of him? Indeed, did the massive mountain still hold him? The mystery of his sheer disappearance perplexed everyone.

Day four commenced with yet another concentrated search effort. Perhaps we had overlooked an important clue. With resignation, the spotter plane and a large contingent of climbers again attacked the peak, aware that this would be their final effort. No member of a rescue team ever envisions ending such an operation unsuccessfully. Driven by sheer determination, each man there was compelled to put forth his last, best effort.

Around noon, a group of us were crisscrossing a steep pitch of cliffs a mere fifty yards below the summit. Suddenly, I noticed a glint coming from a nearby patch of shale. I first suspected that it was merely the bright sun reflecting off wet rock. But, on closer examination, the reflection turned out to be a pair of eye glasses. I gasped. Reaching for them, I noted the lenses were scratched but intact. In a swift exchange of radio communication with Wilson's father at the base camp, the gentleman confirmed that the glasses, indeed, fit the description of those David wore. He also noted that his son was very nearsighted and commented that he would be quite handicapped without them.

The initial excitement over the discovery now compounded the mystery surrounding the search. Clearly, this new evidence indicated that our climber was compromised. We had examined every possible cliff, niche, and boulder field on the west slope of the mountain as well as nearby peaks. If Wilson had made it down from

Lloyd Parratt stands near a trail at Logan Pass. In the background lies the steep west face of Going-to-the-Sun Mountain, the site of the rescue effort.

the summit, he most certainly would have encountered the maintained trail below. Could he have fallen and then made his way down to the scrub timber? Both search and spotter crews combed the area one more time. Nothing.

Another terrifying thought. This was prime grizzly bear country. Could the injured climber have encountered one of the powerful beasts? No evidence of bear activity had been noted during the entire search.

We saw none of the telltale burrows that would show any recent foraging in the mountain meadows. There were no droppings to indicate a bear's presence. Creek beds and overhanging vegetation were carefully checked up to the lush subalpine meadow of Preston Park, where grizzlies often roamed.

And yet, another possibility remained in this mystery. Perhaps Wilson, after losing his glasses, had wandered to the eastern flank of Going-to-the-Sun Mountain. If so, an abrupt drop of several hundred feet could have plunged him into the bergshrund of Sexton Glacier, a large gap between the vertical face of a mountain and the body of ice that makes up the glacier. The patrol plane had circled and its crew had peered down into the void time and again. Nothing. Expert climbers had also carefully scanned the glacier's many crevasses.

With considerable remorse, we left the mountain on Friday, July 31. Thus ended one of the most comprehensive and costly search efforts to date in Glacier National Park's history.

The following day, David Wilson's father, accompanied by park service officials, hiked up a portion of the trail circling the base of Going-to-the-Sun. There, he looked upward and bade an emotional farewell to his son. Planning a return to his home in Maryland the next day, the father made known his appreciation for the extensive search efforts by the park service.

A Blackfeet legend tells how their Sun God, Napi came, in person, to assist the tribe during a time of great need. When his mission was completed, Napi returned to his home in the sun. As he approached the great cliffs at the summit of Going-to-the-Sun Mountain, Napi paused, then disappeared into the clouds.

Since that time, Blackfeet teachings tells us the route Napi followed is the one taken by a person when he dies. Perhaps David Wilson was aware of this legend. To this day, the mystery of his disappearance lingers, its secret known only to the great mountain and perhaps, to Napi, as well.

22
WICKED WANDA

August 1963 – Many Glacier

The military surplus Jeep fire engine gleamed in the sunlight near the front of the large mechanic's stall at park service's Saint Mary headquarters. I had been given a lift from Many Glacier to pick up the shiny red truck after its early summer tune up and mechanical check. Parked in a stall beside our small fire cache, the imposing red vehicle definitely commanded the attention of passersby.

Gil O'Hare placed one foot on the running board of the fire truck and drawled, "She's ready for you...engine runs good, but you're gonna need patience with the pump unit. It's a balky one, but it works most of the time." By anyone's estimate, Gil O'Hare was an excellent mechanic. This particular fire truck had simply been problematic for some time.

Gil had examined the vehicle on several occasions the previous summer due to ongoing problems with its pump. And it must be said that he did his best to repair the temperamental unit each time it rolled into his work bay. A navy veteran, the gentle, patient mechanic kept the vast east side park service fleet running smoothly.

It was my fourth summer serving as fire guard at Many Glacier Ranger Station. At twenty-one, I cherished my solitary position and took my responsibilities seriously. It was my job to make sure the fire engine was always ready for action and looking good. On any given day, I could be seen cleaning and polishing the rig. I had to admit I was proud of it, despite its unpredictable nature.

The Jeep was twenty-five feet in length with a full complement of fire hoses, ladders, fire tools and fire packs. Atop the rear was a one-hundred gallon water tank intended for a quick put down of small fires. The truck's actual pump unit was bolted to an extended front bumper. The centrifugal pump worked off the engine and was controlled by a front-mounted throttle and priming lever. The pump, itself, worked beautifully, quickly exhausting the water supply in the onboard water tank. Once that was gone, a stout eight foot intake hose could be attached to the front of the unit, then dropped into a creek or lake to suck water through the pump and into the fire hoses for hours at a time...or at least, that was the plan. But, unfortunately, this was generally the point where the problems would begin.

My boss, Many Glacier ranger, Larry Dale, and I tested the fire truck's readiness and pumping abilities at least twice a week. The nearest water access was Swiftcurrent Creek, a short drive east from the camp store. Things would inevitably go well until we'd place the intake hose into the stream and begin pumping operations. The pump would sputter a few times and abruptly shudder to a halt. With reservations, the following day, we would again put it to the test and it would, more often than not, work perfectly.

In frustration, we dubbed the truck, *Wicked Wanda*. When questioned, we estimated that the pump would prime and permit suction from the creek about half the time. Headquarters reported that such an efficiency level was probably sufficient and we were encouraged to work with the unit on a more regular basis. The point was also made that we were fortunate just to have a fire truck. In response, Larry responded, dryly, "Guess we have no choice. We'll just do our best with old Wanda then." I was less than encouraged, but, having no say in the matter, I went along with his decision.

August was warm and dry and, so far, we'd been fortunate to experience only test runs with Wanda. Long, quiet summer days stretched uneventfully before us. Then, it happened. One extremely hot afternoon, the call came in from Saint Mary headquarters, "The Babb dump is on fire and its flames are working their way through the grasslands nearby. We need your unit to assist the Saint Mary truck along with two wildland pumper units from the Bureau of Indian Affairs." Although Babb was outside the park on Blackfeet Reservation land, there was the distinct possibility the fire could spread. Certainly, this was reason enough to extinguish it as quickly as possible.

This is what we'd waited for. I hit the ignition switch and Wanda's engine sprang to life. Larry Dale jumped in beside me and we were off. With siren wailing and lights flashing, we roared out of the fire shed and headed down the park road that skirted the shores of Lake Sherburne. Larry and I had worked with Wanda for three summers now. At last, we finally had a chance to fight our first real fire.

Speeding along the straightaway, Wanda's screaming engine peaked out at an astonishing fifty-four miles per hour. Remembering her quirky handling characteristics, I slowed for each of the many tiresome curves in the road. Wanda did not like curves. She wallowed and creaked as we made our way toward Babb, as if to rebel at the very idea of being put to the test by a genuine fire. The radio squawked above the noise of the engine. Three larger units had already arrived at the fire scene. Just ahead, a large plume of smoke came into view. This was it.

We pulled off the park road onto a steep, rocky side road. Stopping briefly, I threw Wanda into four wheel drive. Beautiful. I heard the gears mesh smoothly as she crawled up the bumpy slope, at last reaching the edge of the fire. Soon, we realized, to our dismay, there was very little flame left to be seen. Sadly, Wanda was relegated to mopping up the remaining hot spots in the smoldering grasses. Falling into our familiar drill, we engaged the pump and ran out the water from the onboard tank. Wanda functioned like clockwork. Within five minutes, we'd completely exhausted the tank's water supply. The fire commander radioed us to move our unit over to the edge of a nearby creek to access the water there in order to continue our pumping operation.

The engine labored as we clambered over large rocks, picking our way across the final stretch which led to the creek. Upon reaching the stream, Larry jumped out, attaching and then dropping the large suction hose into the swirling waters. After putting the truck in neutral, I ran to the front to assist him with the pump unit. Pushing up the engine's throttle knob, I threw the priming lever into gear. No

Wicked Wanda sparkles outside the Many Glacier Ranger Station.

response. Nothing. Frustrated, I pushed the lever back and forth repeatedly. Once again, Wanda's pump refused to prime. Larry joined me, giving it a try himself. Again, nothing. The fire hose lay there immobile. Larry blurted, "Damn. Wouldn't you know it? The one time we really need her to pump, she won't." I bowed my head in disgust and pounded the hood.

Larry hit the radio button to report that our unit's pump was disabled. Covered in black soot from the fire and sweating profusely in the hot sun, we wound up the hose and made a bumpy retreat back to the park road. Wanda had died on us and everybody in the park would soon hear about it. How humiliating.

At summer's end, the temperamental Wanda, was, at last, taken out of service with the promise of a new unit to take her place. With all due respect, I hope, somewhere out there, Wicked Wanda rests in peace.

23

NEWLYWEDS AND
BEAR TRAPS

During the era spanning the 1950's through the 1970's, the park service family at Saint Mary could be called a tightly knit group. Each summer, seasonal employees, several with families, made the June trek from their assorted home states to Glacier for the visitor season. Many returned to the park for a succession of summers, forging lifelong friendships in the process. The staffs of rangers, ranger naturalists and park maintenance people were often teachers who used the summer break to work in this spectacular setting.

The excitement grew in early June, as the bonds of many summers past were rekindled. Each time a familiar vehicle arrived at the housing area, gleeful shouts could be heard. Warm welcomes rang out as old friends were reunited once again.

A collection of cabins, apartments and trailers provided living quarters for the ninety day wonders, as seasonals often humorously called themselves. Within a week's time, everyone had arrived and their varied summer activities began.

Long distance grocery shopping safaris to Kalispell, group hikes, fishing expeditions, huckleberry picking and potluck suppers were all greatly enjoyed. But, perhaps the most unique activity was the *shivaree*. A French word, the shivaree refers to a "noisy, mock serenade for newlyweds."

If a member of the park service family had married since the previous summer, such a celebration was in order. The playful event involved newlyweds, a bear trap, a crowd and the element of surprise. A day or two before the shivaree, one of the park's bear traps would be quietly brought to a secluded location near park housing. Children, eager to be a part of the spoof, were easily recruited to clean the trap's interior. Following this distasteful chore, they took great delight in decorating the strange contraption.

The common bear trap used in a national park setting is constructed of a section of metal culvert mounted atop a trailer. Metal rods crisscross front and back ends of the culvert trap, one end housing the entrance. A baited release hook hangs at the end farthest from a trap door. When the tempting scent of the bait reaches a bear, it is lured into the trap. Then, with a tug at the baited hook, the entry door releases, trapping the bear inside.

After a few hours' captivity, the traps were rank with the odor of bear waste. Cleaning a bear trap for a shivaree demanded hard work but, armed with brushes and lots of soapy water, the children met the task with enthusiasm. They reveled in the prank that would soon take place as a result of their clandestine efforts.

Generally, a newly married pair realized their shivaree was inevitable, but the date and the time of this event was a mystery. In one instance, a newlywed couple

A group of park service children decorate a bear trap for a Shivaree.

drove into the housing complex, weary and hungry after an overnight hike in Glacier's backcountry. With no signs of life to be seen, the puzzled couple pulled to a stop and sat in their car for several moments. Suddenly, a shout was heard as gleeful friends

Half the fun was making signs for the bear trap used in the shivaree. Smitty, at age eleven, is second from the right.

converged on the pair from every direction. Reluctantly, the couple was pried from their car and led to the bear trap. Once inside, the heavy metal door clanged shut and the shivaree began.

In the lively parade that followed, a fire engine took the lead with its siren blaring and red lights flashing. Close behind came the bear trap, with its captive humans, tin cans clattering noisily in its wake. Pickup trucks, patrol cars and family autos followed, horns honking loudly. Slowly, the procession made its way out of the housing area and proceeded to Saint Mary village. Tourists gawked as the strange parade wended its way around the lodge and then through the campgrounds. Onlookers quickly realized the bear trap and its soccupants were the parade's center of interest. Signs attached to the trap proclaimed, "Just Married" and "The Trapped Family."

At last, the procession returned home and the couple was released. A short time later, they were honored at a festive barbecue, held near the shores of Saint Mary Lake.

1964 marked my final summer's work in Glacier. Then, a fireguard at Saint Mary, I witnessed a shivaree as a cheering participant. Reflecting upon my many treasured summers within this remarkable place, it seems fitting that its strong bonds and traditions still evoke fond memories. For, not only were our surroundings almost sacred in their beauty, but the friendships forged there have lasted a lifetime.

EPILOGUE

The stories in this book were written with the aid of personal journals, the guidance of family members, time spent interviewing retired park service employees and the author's memory of events past. As boys, Monty and I regarded our summers in Glacier as one continual adventure. Monty stood by his belief that there was absolutely nothing he would change about this perfect place. In spite of his horrific bear mauling, Smitty insists that he would change none of his Glacier experiences. An intense affection for Glacier's remarkable wilderness resides in the hearts of the entire Parratt family.

I am convinced that our parents, Lloyd and Grace, could have chosen a civilized and predictable lifestyle for their sons by spending summers at their home in southern California. Working there, day to day, would have netted greater financial gain. Fortunately, both were adventurers at heart with a keen appreciation for the beauty and wonder to be found in nature. Consequently, they chose to explore Yosemite and, finally, Glacier National Park during their summer breaks from teaching. They and their sons to follow, came to know the rewards of a passionate love for this wild place, a love so intense as to become part of one's very heart and spirit.

As we grew, each of the Parratt boys came to regard their summers in Glacier as wondrous gifts, unselfishly provided by their loving parents. Dad worked as a ranger naturalist in this great park from 1945 through 1965. Obvious to all who knew him was the great affection he held for his family, his work, and his Glacier.

Monty and I appreciated our parents' trust in us which allowed us to explore, at will, areas far beyond our beloved Sun Camp Ranger Station. We knew the freedom of experiencing, first hand, Glacier's beautiful, yet occasionally unforgiving nature. With Dad's guidance, we quickly learned what he liked to call wilderness smarts.

As several of the stories illustrate, some of our most poignant life lessons were, indeed, learned by trial and error. Many stories reflect the grave danger and trauma encountered by the Parratt family in this wild place. Looking back, Smitty and I confess that many of the lessons learned in Glacier help us face challenges we encounter in our lives today.

The rigors of the Glacier experience helped to build strong character in the Parratt brothers as we made our transitions from boys to young men. Even after we were compelled to leave this paradise for college, then marriage, work and the business of raising families, we've continued to return to Glacier Park to recharge physically and spiritually. Each time we behold this hallowed place, deep emotions stir. I cannot view the shoreline of Upper Saint Mary Lake where our family cabin stood without shedding tears of joy, recalling the happiness we knew there. To each one of us, this is a holy place unlike any other.

You may ask, "What became of the Parratt family after their summers in Glacier ended?" My own experiences can be found in the section of the book entitled, *About the Author*. I would like to add a comment of interest which relates to Kay Dell, my wonderful wife of eight years. Kay Dell was married, at one time, to Alan Nelson, a major principal in the Otokomi grizzly bear attack. Due to life's circumstances, we found ourselves single some ten years ago. Having met in Glacier the summer of 1960, we were able to reconnect thirty-eight years later through the marvel of e-mail. The rest, as they say, is history!

Monty worked on Glacier's blister rust crew from 1963 to 1967. He served as a crew foreman and was involved in numerous mountain rescues. He also helped fight several noteworthy forest fires. While attending Whitworth College, he earned the honor of small college All-American during an illustrious football career. It was on this campus that he also met his love, Laurel Lundgren, of West Glacier, Montana.

Laurel and Monty were married in 1967 and both enjoyed long and productive teaching careers in Marysville, Washington. In

Baby Smitty in an old-fashioned stroller.

addition to his teaching, Monty was a coach who positively affected the lives of countless youth. He championed the efforts of students and athletes, often helping bring success to the shunned and underprivileged. He was loved and respected by students and teachers alike. Al Frutel, a colleague, stated, "Monty was probably one of the finest men who ever walked the face of the earth." Each summer, our brother made many trips to Glacier to share its beauty with his family and countless friends. In the wake of his untimely death in 2001, the Marysville School District named the Totem Middle School gymnasium after him, an honor befitting a great man. To this day, it is said, the name Monty Parratt is legendary to many in the Glacier Park he loved.

Smitty is the epitome of a survival success story. After excelling in college, he ultimately married his soul mate, Shawn Kilpatric. Together, they chose careers with the National Park Service, working in a number of locations throughout the country. Smitty retired in 2008 after a long and successful tenure as a master interpretive naturalist. The couple moved from their most recent assignment in Alaska's Wrangell Saint Elias National Park and Preserve to Crater Lake National Park in Oregon.

Shawn continues her career as a budget analyst while Smitty pursues his teaching aspirations at two colleges near their home in Chiloquin. The same indomitable will which allowed him to survive the horrific bear mauling continues to propel Smitty through a life rich with world travel and adventure. His determination and stamina, coupled with an extraordinary intellect, have shaped the active and fulfilling lifestyle he shares with Shawn.

Lloyd and Grace Parratt have shed their earthly bonds but hold special places in our hearts and our memories. In large part, we owe our successes in life to our remarkable parents. Our adventures during Glacier's glory days forged the living spirit which will forever bind the hearts of the Parratt family.

ABOUT THE AUTHOR

Mark Parratt was born in 1941 in Cleveland, Ohio. He was raised in California where his parents worked as educators. The Parratt family spent eighteen consecutive summers in Glacier National Park, Montana, where his father took employment as a seasonal ranger naturalist. While growing up as young boys, Mark and his brothers Monty and Smitty took great delight in exploring the many wonders of Glacier. These adventures, paired with his eventual work with the park service, allowed the author to intimately experience the many faces of Glacier from her stark beauty to her sometimes unforgiving nature. Following college and a Fulbright Scholarship to Australia, Mark held the position of Professor of Botany and Environmental Biology at Fullerton College in Fullerton, California. His thirty-three year tenure included publication of his textbook, *Environmental Biology*, which ran several editions. He and his wife, Kay Dell, now divide their time between southern California and Montana. They continue to visit Glacier Park at every opportunity.

Mark and Kay Dell Parratt.
Photograph courtesy Colleen Darrow Browning.

LaVergne, TN USA
12 March 2010
175800LV00001B/171/P